Oleana

THE OLE BULL COLONY

BY

PAUL W. HEIMEL

Publisher:

KNOX Books
407 Mill Street
Coudersport PA 16915
(814) 274-9493

ISBN 0-9655824-2-6

First edition, August 2002
Printed in Canada

Cover design by Deb Craven
(Cable Television Services Inc., Boulder, Colo.)
Layout and graphic art by Joseph A. Majot
Photographer/Photo Consultant: Robert Gerlach II

Additional copies available from: www.olebull.org

Also from Knox Books:

Eliot Ness: The Real Story (ISBN 0-9655824-0-X)
The true story of America's most famous crimefighter.

Dedication

To my wife and life's partner, Lugene;
to my family
for the unconditional love and understanding
during my time "away."

Oleana

To the Reader

Hidden behind the thickets and thornapples, the tall trees and the scattered signs of modern civilization at Oleana, in the rugged mountains of northcentral Pennsylvania, lies a cemetery where tombstones with timeworn lettering have tumbled to ground. They take their place beside smooth, faceless rocks that protrude awkwardly from the soil, final testament to lives that have been lost and—in some cases—forgotten. Nearby, a mountain stream flows southward toward the Atlantic Ocean, just as it has for thousands of years.

This is the graveyard of "New Norway," known more commonly in recent years simply as *Oleana*. Buried beneath are the hopes and dreams of a generation of Norwegians who believed in the great Ole Bull and his power to transform their lives.

In order to understand the essence of Oleana, it is necessary to gain an appreciation for Ole Bull— the man, the character and the legend. His special personality and appeal are what give the story its significance.

As the Oleana story unfolded, its developments were watched with great interest in Norway by conservatives fearing the worst about emigration, by country folk seeking a better life and by those who were merely interested in Ole Bull because of his celebrity status.

At the same time, the colony was of considerable interest to American leaders who sought to exploit the growing numbers of European immigrants arriving in the country with an eagerness to work, and to others who were captivated by Bull's undeniable charisma.

The purpose of this book is to recreate the colony as thoroughly and accurately as possible some 150 years after its rapid rise and fall. Additionally, to give the story context, this work examines the life of Ole Bull, the causes and effects of emigration, the reasons for the colony's failure, the public's reaction in the United States and Norway and the fate of the colonists.

A series of challenges confronts anyone who researches Oleana. There are only scattered transcripts of interviews with eyewitnesses. Newspapers, magazines and books of yesteryear did not employ the same standards of objectivity, thoroughness or accuracy. Misconceptions and false assumptions have grown to mythical proportions with the passage of time.

One can only imagine the special quality of Ole Bull's violin playing. While countless music critics and journalists verify his performing excellence, there are no recordings. Many of his greatest compositions have been lost or destroyed; of those that survive today, some require orchestration or a performer's own interpretation to bring them to life.

Further aggravating the research is the division that has deepened between the two branches of descendants, stemming from Bull's first and second marriages, and the fact that certain individuals claiming close kinship with one or the other branch have promoted tales with no basis in fact.

A decade ago, I studied the Oleana colony in some detail and authored the book *Shattered Dreams: The Oleana Colony in Pennsylvania* (Leader Publishing, Coudersport, Pa., 1992). Little did I know then that my work had barely scratched the surface.

In the ensuing years, additional information emerged, allowing me to position more pieces into the puzzle. Then, in 2000, another writer and follower of the Oleana story, Paul Engelstad from the Washington D.C. area, paid me a call. He shared with me volumes of material he had discovered during his many years of retracing Ole Bull's footsteps in both Norway and this country.

We agreed that the full story had not yet been told, and he agreed to share what he had found in order for me to tell it. Many people in Norway and the United States have been helpful and supportive. Without that assistance and without Paul Engelstad's treasure of translated interviews, obscure newspaper clippings and other documents, this book would not have been possible.

Paul W. Heimel
Coudersport, Pa.
June 2002

Introduction

"Come to our 'New Norway' in Pennsylvania, where you'll find a warm heart and a helpful hand," said the distinguished-looking gentleman who greeted passengers as they milled on the deck of the ship, *Incognito*, soon after it dropped anchor in New York harbor in September 1852.

Some of them recognized him; many of those who didn't know him by sight surely knew his name. He was Ole Bull, a revered national hero, to whom the music and cultural traditions of Norway were a passion. He beckoned passengers who came to America seeking freedom and economic improvement to join his settlement.

A pyrotechnic performer, Bull brought pride and fame to Norway while symbolizing independence and an element of irreverence— perhaps even frivolity. He was a romantic in the truest sense, and was generally acknowledged as the world's foremost violinist, following in the footsteps of Italy's legendary Nicolo Paganini. Bull had captivated concert crowds with a repertoire that mixed classics by Mozart, Beethoven and other greats with his own compositions, often weaving into his program more contemporary selections familiar to the listeners. Music critics hailed him for his performing ability, even as they railed him for appealing to the commoners and the musically unschooled. Bull, however, felt no obligation to bow to their elitist demands. Concert appearances, sometimes announced only a day or two in advance, would regularly sell out and rarely fail to please.

Oleana

Bull was a conspicuous visitor to New York, and not just to Norwegians. He had taken America by storm during an 1843-45 tour that covered most of the major cities. The concert series made him a wealthy man and introduced him to the vast landscape and resources of this developing land. He was struck by America's spirit and seemingly limitless possibilities. With this in mind, nearly a decade later he came back to America not to perform, but to build a colony. His mission was to persuade thousands of his countrymen to populate his "New Norway," where they could live under the cloak of American freedom and the promise of a comfortable quality of life.

Economics, more than any other factors, had motivated the *Incognito* passengers to leave Norway and settle in the New World. Their modest, marginally productive farms had been made even smaller as they were divided among growing families under a government-protected system that granted property rights with the inherent responsibilities to first-born sons.

The lack of jobs both on and off the farms made life hard, especially for those between the ages of 20 and 30. The promise of land and opportunity through homesteading, fueled by reports from early emigrants to the United States, was a powerful lure. Scores of Norwegians were setting sail for America. Thousands of others wished they could.

Most of the passengers on the *Incognito* were originally bound for the early Scandinavian settlements in Wisconsin and Minnesota. However, the symbolic attraction and persuasive powers of Ole Bull, the incentives he offered, and the glowing descriptions of his Pennsylvania lands— said to be similar to their native Norway— were an irresistible combination.

Millions of years before man, dense forests covered the mountain range that would become known as the Alleghenies. Scattered bands of Native Americans from the Delaware tribe passed through this unbroken landscape of native pine, hemlock and cherry trees that held little allure as a home. They preferred the more flat and open land to grow their crops. Archeological digs suggest the Delawares did establish temporary encampments in these mountains, evidently to harvest the abundant wildlife while seeking more suitable lands for settlement.

Explorers and an occasional missionary passed through the region in the 1700s. Behind them came the speculators hired by wealthy men and large land companies seeking to expand their domains.

The first permanent settlers arrived during the early 19th century. A roughly rectangular land mass positioned in the middle of Pennsylvania's northern border with New York State was officially declared Potter County in 1804, in honor of General James Potter, who served under George Washington during the American Revolution. Several towns were surveyed and named in the northern sections of Potter County, while the more mountainous terrain to the south where Bull would build his colony remained unsettled.

The early pioneers experienced continual trials and hardships. Forestland was thick and not easily cleared for farming. Supplies of food and other necessities were far away, and not easily accessible. Wolves, panthers and black bears were constant menaces and the harsh winters took their toll. But the early pioneers gradually won their battles against the elements. Roads were blazed, log cabins built, gristmills, sawmills and other developments established, and by 1810 spotted sections of Potter County became home to more than 100 settlers.

In this same year, half a globe away in the coastal city of Bergen, Norway, Johan and Anna Bull welcomed into the world their son Ole, the first of ten children.

One

Ole Bornemann Bull was born on Feb. 5, 1810, in his parents' residence above the family's pharmacy on Strandgatan Street. This was one of the city's finer homes, distinguishable by a white swan of wood that hung over the entrance.

Johan Storm Bull, like his father before him, was a respected chemist and apothecary. On Oct. 23, 1809, he married Anna Dorothea Borse Geelmuyden, the daughter of an attorney, Knud Geelmuyden, and Anna Margrethe Munthe. The Geelmuydens had arrived in Bergen from Holland around 1660. Income from the pharmacy business allowed the Bulls to enjoy a standard of living above that of many Bergensers.

A picturesque city built compactly on the rocky coast of the North Sea in western Norway, Bergen was—and still is—a busy commercial and trading center, its harbor packed with boats of many varieties and its colorful homes contrasting notably from the surroundings. That harbor sometimes resembles a fairyland as the colorful sunsets and rocky mountaintops are reflected in the sea. German Hanseatic merchants dominated much of the commerce there, a situation that generated resentment among the natives. Because the harbor was open to England, Germany, Iceland and other nations, Bergen's population was as diverse as any Scandinavian city.

Bergensers have always considered themselves different from other Norwegians: adventurous and lively, free of pretensions, sometimes quick-tempered and fiercely independent. They are thought to have mannerisms all their own, a distinctive dialect and a reputation for friendliness and helpfulness to visitors. In Bergen, patriotism is measured by one's loyalty not only to Norway, but even more so to the city itself.

Both of his parents and several other family members were amateur musicians, so early in life, Ole Bull witnessed the pleasure and inspiration that could be derived from performing. Family and friends often gathered at the Bull home to perform string music. Bergen boasted its own orchestra and a theater had opened there in 1790, but culture was barely making in-roads in a city where commercialism and material values dominated the life and thinking of the people. It has been written that young Ole, whisked off to bed by his parents, tiptoed down to the foot of the stairs to sit and listen as the adults performed the compositions of Beethoven, Haydn, Mozart and others.

Ole Bull is also said to have heard music in the sounds of nature, just as he imagined musical background to the tales his grandmother would tell of trolls and gnomes in the Norwegian mountains. His abilities drew the attention of his uncle, Jens Geelmuyden, a newspaper editor and cellist, who bought a child's size violin for Ole.

Impressed that the boy could play rudimentary melodies almost immediately, Geelmuyden persuaded his sister to allow Ole to stay up late while the family musicians and their friends performed. Ole's mother taught him how to read music and play the piano at the same time he learned how to read and write. His father preached the value of education, perhaps owing to Johan Bull's own status among Bergen's educated, cultivated class.

Ole, for his part, preferred to interact with the common folks in Bergen. Self-confident and mischievous as a child, he sometimes skipped school to climb the rocky mountains, walk in the woods, watch the ships, or listen to the seamen's tales of countries far away. The rugged dockworkers took a liking to this firm, sturdy boy of fair Norwegian complexion, large brown eyes and straight light brown hair.

Childhood summers were spent about 10 miles northeast of Bergen at the family's summer compound on the island of Osteroy, where Johan Bull's mother lived in a modest home known as Valestrand, which means "whale beach." She often entertained him with traditional folktales and ballads. Ole could wander outside and within minutes be mingling with the colorful natives who worked the farms or tended to the fishermen's latest catches. He also explored the jagged coastline and watched the turbulent North Sea as it thrust itself into the long, narrow fjords lined by gray mountains, or he could climb the hillside trails to witness the sights and sounds of nature or play in the river that ran behind the house.

During this same period, Bull was exposed to the Hardanger fiddle, a special west Norwegian violin with underlying sympathetic drone strings. Bridal processions with colorful costumes occasionally would pass the Valestrand estate, fiddlers leading the way. Fascinated by these characters, Ole began to imitate them on his own violin, to the amazement of his family.

Johan Bull yielded to the pressure of his wife and brother-in-law, purchasing a violin for Ole and enrolling him in music lessons at the age of eight. This was an adult-sized violin, prompting some biographers to speculate that it was too large for him, resulting in Bull's peculiar way of holding his instrument throughout the rest of his life. Two instructors attempted to teach him the basics, but Bull was impatient and obstinent. The fact that his teachers, let alone his parents, often allowed Ole's tantrums to go unpunished may have contributed to his lack of discipline or conformity later in life. No one contested his brilliance as a performer, yet his reluctance to master the theoretical aspects of music handicapped him throughout his career.

Some say Bull lacked the discipline to commit some of his greatest solo works to paper, or to complete the orchestrations that would have made his music more acceptable to archivists and critics. There are also reports that Bull destroyed some of his compositions during fits of anger or frustration over what he perceived as their shortcomings.

On the other hand, because he did not always conform to the limits of the written page, Bull was able to explore his own creative abilities.

He practiced for hours at a time. Taking his fiddle into the woods and the mountains, he would listen to the wind in the trees, the roar of the sea, the singing and chattering of birds and other sounds of nature, then imitate them on his instrument and compose ditties based on them. These influences were acknowledged by Bull himself, in conversations with Professor Rasmus Anderson, a strong promoter of Norwegian culture and friend of Bull's during the latter's late adulthood:

I once asked Ole Bull what had inspired his weird and original melodies. His answer was that from his earliest childhood he had taken the profoundest delight in Norway's natural scenery. He grew eloquent in his poetic description of the grand and picturesque flower-clad valleys, filled with soughing groves and singing birds; of the silver-crested mountains, from which the summer sun never departs; of the melodious brooks, babbling streams, and thundering rivers; of the blinking lakes that sink deep thoughts to starlit skies; of the far-penetrating fjords and the many thousand islands on the coast.

He spoke with special emphasis of the eagerness with which he had devoured all myths, folk-tales, ballads and other melodies; and all these things, he said, "have made my music." And we would emphasize the fact that these things made his music, not alone by their influence upon his mind, but also by the impression they made upon several generations of his ancestors who have contemplated them.

Sometimes at Valestrand, Ole and his younger brothers would comb the beach, selecting seashells of different tones to blow upon under Ole's direction.

As difficult a music student as he was, the passion of Bull's performing was not lost on his instructors. Technical brilliance and a warm melodic line emerged, whether he was creating his own music or elaborating on established themes. At age eight, Bull was admitted to the local orchestra at Bergen.

Bull's respect for the work of the legendary Italian composer and violinist Niccolo Paganini bordered on worship. At his career peak, Bull would be favorably compared to his idol. A few critics hailed him as superior, perhaps caught up in the emotion of the moment—for it is well documented that Ole Bull could stir the emotions. Even if Bull was as skillful a performer as Paganini, he will never rank with Liszt, Chopin, Mendelssohn or the other great composers of his day.

Ole Bull was sent to a Latin school, but failed to demonstrate the interest or the discipline necessary to survive academically. Conflicts were inevitable. Some biographical accounts tell of a physical skirmish between Bull—now a tall, attractive and solid young man—and his tutor, leading the latter to ease his demand that Bull attend to his studies more and play his violin less. As resistant as Ole was to structured education, he prided himself on his knowledge of Odin, Thor and other mythological figures as well as Norwegian folklore. His musical education took a major step forward when Ole became a student of K. Mathias Lundholm. This renowned Swedish violinist and former conductor taught Bull both the French and German traditions of violin playing.

Johan and Anna Bull resigned themselves to the fact that their first-born would never be a druggist, a scientist or a great scholar. They insisted that their 18-year-old son enroll at the University of Christiania, located in the capital city of Norway, to study religion and prepare for a life as a Lutheran clergyman. That plan was doomed from the start, as Bull failed his entrance exam in Latin. A despondent Ole wrote his parents: "What has happened has happened, and I hope you won't reproach me for it. If fate had been more favorable, who knows what it may be good for?"

He remained in Christiania, entertaining university students with his violin and soon performing under the direction of Waldemar Thrane, Norway's leading composer and conductor of the Christiana Orchestra. Thrane recognized Bull's skills and welcomed the youngster into his orchestra. A few months later, upon Thrane's premature death, Bull became the orchestra's conductor.

Two

Individuality and a certain amount of non-conformance would be recurring themes in the life of Ole Bull. In the capital city he found a natural ally in Henrik Wergeland, soon to become one of Norway's most famous literary figures and a fervent advocate of political freedom and national independence. Bull and Wergeland shared a deep devotion to Norwegian culture and a strong resentment of the continued intrusion into their nation by its neighbors Sweden and Denmark.

Norway's dynastic union with Denmark from 1450 to 1814 had led to the dominance of the more populous country. Norway's secondary status—"the stepchild of Scandinavia"—was symbolized by the renaming of the capital city, Oslo, as Christiania in 1624, after the Danish King Christian IV. Because Norway had no royal house of its own, it lacked the music and culture that typically thrived in court circles. Music still played an important role in the religious centers, however, and town musicians provided entertainment, while folk music flourished freely in the countryside.

Centuries of Danish rule officially ended in 1814, when the country became united with Sweden under a joint king, enjoying autonomy but not independence. The leaders of the Norwegian nation drafted and adopted a constitution based on American and French examples, but the union with Sweden kept Norwegians from realizing the freedoms set forth in their constitution.

They were divided between "pro-Scandinavians" and "patriots." Among the patriots, cultural figures such as Ole Bull and Henrik Wergeland aroused a strong desire for total independence. Meanwhile, Wergeland's ardent interest in Norwegian folk tunes laid the groundwork for a national music tradition. Norwegians preserved their ballads, their popular melodies, their folklore and their legends. Economically, however, they continued to struggle.

Dating as far back as the 16th century, Europeans had heard reports of explorers and mapmakers who described the "New World." The realities of this land that would become America meant little to them until they read the firsthand narratives of those who survived the perils of the Atlantic journeys and saw for themselves what this new land was like.

As the forces of emigration swept through the Norwegian countryside in the early 1800s, letters from across the sea were read with absorbed interest and made available to the newspapers. To those who had the means and the resolve, emigration posed a choice between two worlds.

Correspondence known at the time as "America letters" sparked an impulse to emigrate, which was also given a name: "America fever." These letters were filled with contrasts springing from idealistic hopes and realistic disappointments. For every tale of success and excitement there was one of disillusionment and suffering.

In addition to informing Europeans of the conditions in the New World, these letters were perhaps the most effective single factor in bringing discontent to a focus and into action. America, though not a utopia, offered land, opportunity and hope that were denied or rigidly limited in the Norwegian old order.

In the midst of this rising tide of nationalism and romanticism, the 1825 sailing of the ship "Restoration," with 52 passengers aboard, from the Stavanger harbor on Norway's southwest coast marked the beginning of Norwegian group migration to America. Greeted upon their arrival at the port of New York by Cleng Peerson, the passengers settled in Kendall Township, N. Y., on the shores of Lake Ontario. To some extent, Peerson's story mirrors that of Ole Bull. For many years he encouraged Norwegians to sail for America in order to escape their native land's hardships— particularly fishermen's drownings, rising prices for farmland and an extended drought.

This spirit of restlessness and opposition to the established order was not lost upon Ole Bull and many other young people in Christiania. On May 17, 1829, Bull joined Wergeland during an independence celebration that was rudely interrupted by a cavalry troop. Wergeland was among those who were injured in the melee. The 17th of May has been celebrated as Constitution Day with great enthusiasm ever since.

Christiania was too far removed from Europe's expanding musical climate for Bull's liking. Henrik Wergeland wrote: "He was not at rest in Christiania. His mind was in a state of restless agitation. He was like a balloon straining and tugging to get loose from its moorings and rise into the upper air."

Bull left for Cassel, Germany, to seek advice and criticism from Louis Spohr, a highly respected violin teacher, orchestra conductor, solo performer and composer. Much to Bull's chagrin, Spohr refused to accept him as a student. Spohr's strict adherence to the written music of his era—with little room for deviation or improvisation—suggests that the two would likely have clashed anyhow. Bull could master the classics with the best of performers, but his forte was his personal expression and innovation. He had begun to employ mechanical devices, such as lowering the bridge of his violin or using an extremely long and heavy bow, to create his own sound. These techniques, sometimes labeled trickery by his detractors, combined with his outstanding performing skills made the young Norwegian a true phenomenon. By the summer of 1829, Bull was impressing German audiences with his rapid fire staccato and double-, or even quadruple-stopping.

Ole Bull returned to Christiana to find that his reputation had grown. He spent most of the next two years performing in Norway while saving money that would allow him to visit Paris, which to Bull represented the ultimate in timeless tradition, romance and musical inspiration.

His studies of harmony led him to compose musical accompaniment for two poems by Henrik Wergeland, "Hymn to Freedom" and "Thunder." Wergeland, in a biographical work on Bull, wrote: "Bull was like most geniuses in combining with a melancholy but mobile temperament a most childlike and trustworthy disposition, and differing from them by having still retained it."

A typical day in the life of Ole Bull included practice sessions with two orchestras and private lessons for some pupils, as well as his own practicing, his continuing study of harmony and his composing. This dedication to music was reflected in letters he sent back home. In one, he wrote, "I am not at all well and am very melancholy . . . I am working on a symphony, but as I am almost shy towards people, I am afraid my ideas will be just as shy of people. I often have so much to do that I don't get time to eat. But I still won't give up." Appeals for sympathy would become standard behavior for Ole Bull.

His curiosity about the Hardanger fiddle prompted Bull to seek out one of its most accomplished players, Torgeir Augundson, in the summer of 1831. Augundson, visiting Bergen from his home in Telemark—a region famous for its folklore—accepted Bull's invitation to join him at Valestrand. An attentive Bull wrote down the notes of several Augundson renderings. Passages derived from them would resurface later in Bull's own repertoire as representative of Norwegian folk culture. He soon added a Hardanger to his fiddle collection.

Combining money from his concert tours with contributions from family and friends, Ole bid farewell to his parents, brothers and sisters and shoved off for France. He would not see Norway again for seven years.

Paris was all that Bull expected— and more. It was an ideal atmosphere for any musician. He soon became acquainted with Heinrich Wilhelm Ernst, a respected teenaged violinist who was regularly performing before appreciative audiences. Bull also spent time with Poland's great composer and pianist Frederic Chopin, who at age 21 had just arrived in Paris and was building his own musical reputation. He also befriended Italian composer Giocchino Rossini and other European legends-in-the-making.

What continued to separate Bull from the other greats was his penchant for personal adventure and his stubborn refusal to comply with the traditional rules. "If Ole Bull had gone the right way," wrote the famous German artist Joseph Joachim, "he would have been the greatest of all violinists."

He resisted colleagues' pleas that he enroll at the conservatory in Paris for lessons. Perhaps it was therefore no surprise when he was denied membership in the Paris Opera Orchestra because of his arrogance and limited formal musical education. Bull sometimes reacted with anger and suspicion at any criticism of his work, and his reaction to the orchestra's rejection was no exception.

He often claimed that he was the target of a conspiracy to undermine his career. Grand schemes to exploit him are detailed at length in the book, *Ole Bull: A Memoir*, by his widow, Sara Bull (Houghton Mifflin, 1882). These likely reflect the exaggerated accounts of victimization and self-pity that marked Bull's reminiscences later in life. Yet, Bull displayed a certain charm and joy of life that often conquered his detractors. He spent lavishly on fancy clothes, parties for musician friends, gambling, and violins priced beyond his means.

Now in his early twenties, Bull was asserting his independence. Letters to his parents were less frequent and he lived each day with little apparent regard for the future, regularly in financial difficulty with little support from home. He couldn't be bothered to attend to his health or save money, nor would he commit vast portions of his time to composing. However, the one discipline to which he continued to devote his energies was his advancing skill as a violinist.

Bull rented a room in a Paris boarding house, where he fell ill. While the owner, a widow named Madame Villeminot, was nursing him back to health, Ole found himself strongly attracted to her orphaned 14-year-old granddaughter. The innocent, quiet Alexandrine Felicite Villeminot, commonly known as "Felicie," was likewise smitten by the handsome

Norwegian and rarely left his side.

Once he had recovered, Bull resumed his practicing and composing. He focused most intently on a piece that would become known as "The Mountains of Norway," blending Norwegian folk melodies for the Hardanger fiddle with more complex and traditional classical music components.

The April 1833 arrival of the great Paganini in Paris provided Ole Bull with his first opportunity to see his idol perform. His notes from the show reflect how carefully he studied the Italian master, searching for anything that would help him refine his own skills. The contrast between Paganini's reception in Paris and audiences' reaction to his own work convinced Bull that the French musical establishment did not appreciate his talents.

Several of Europe's great musicians were captivated by the tales of eager audiences and the financial bonanza in the New World. For all of its appeal as a land of independence and economic opportunity, the United States was culturally deprived. Bull read with great interest the accounts of the emigrants who sailed to America, but did not consider himself yet ready to join his rival musicians there. Paganini's reception in Paris may have convinced him that he needed to continue his own professional growth.

Ole was instead bound for Switzerland, still enamored with the young French girl who had helped him to get back on his feet. Bull found Lake Geneva to be reminiscent of Norway and wrote to Felicie that he yearned to live "in this country where one is free as a bird, together with my two dearest women friends, whose names perhaps you know." As he performed in Geneva, Lausanne and Vevey, Bull's reputation grew with each successive appearance. He looked back at the summer of 1833 as his professional breakthrough.

Bull moved on to Italy and found those crowds even more enthusiastic and inspiring. He came under the helpful influence of the greatest soprano of his day, Maria Felicia Malibran, and began writing in the Italian opera style. He composed his "Concerto in A Major" while in

Italy, performing it for the first time with the Philharmonic Society at Bologna. Hearing calls for pieces such as "Norma," "The Siege of Corinth" and "Romeo and Juliet," Bull proceeded to combine excerpts from all three into one improvisational piece, sending the crowd into a frenzy.

From that point forward, he often extracted native folk songs, patriotic tunes or other recognizable melodies from the nation in which he was performing and weaved them into his repertoire. One of his biographers, Mortimer Smith (*The Life of Ole Bull*, Princeton University Press, 1943), wrote:

After Bologna, Ole's successes followed one another with monotonous regularity. Italy did a great deal for the young Ole Bull. Success there added to his confidence, association with nobility ironed out many of his eccentricities of manner and gave him the polish of a gentleman of the world; but primarily Italy colored and shaped the direction in which his musical talent was to develop in the future. The Italians were fond of melody and sentiment and showy effects, and encouraged Ole in his already pronounced leanings toward the same kind of music.

In Italy he composed "Polacca Guerriera" and "Adagio Religioso." The latter, inspired by the friars of Santa Maria Novello at Florence, included the melodic "A Mother's Prayer," a standard that Bull performed throughout the rest of his career. It's one of the few Ole Bull compositions still heard today.

The "Polacca" is a particularly challenging piece involving a finale in which separate parts are played on each of the violin's four strings during a continuous shaking that lasts for 15 bars. Bull's ability to perform the feat with such lightning swiftness, requiring both strength and flexibility, thrilled audiences and music critics alike.

Ole continued to send letters to Felicie. In one of them, he wrote, "I am in the greatest anxiety about you all. If I can be of any service to you, dispose of me and you will give me the greatest pleasure. I will even leave Italy if your welfare requires it, and come to you . . . Keep for me your esteem and friendship, and believe me always your true friend and obedient servant."

All the while, Bull sought out news from Norway, curious about his own reputation and the development of economic, political and social trends in his homeland.

Three

The Ole Bull who set foot in Paris in May 1835 was a different performer than the one who had been so frustrated there a few years earlier. After spending two weeks with Felicie and her grandmother, the 25-year-old Bull emerged to answer the public's call and was immediately embraced. The doors of the Grand Opera, where he had been denied the opportunity to perform, were now open to him.

Bull's reputation had spread throughout French population centers and his performances only confirmed the glowing reviews. The critics were lavish in their praise:

L'Artiste: "Monsieur Bull has made us admire his boldness, his spirit, the wonderful speed of his bow, and purity of his tone, the depth of his feeling and musical thought; and all this without charlatanism, with all the naivete and the simplicity of a genius who sees only his art and believes only in himself."

La Courier des Theatres: "Ole Bull's playing is full of soul and energy, of gentleness and charm . . . He not only showed his skill with difficult pieces, but his violin sang so much expressively that one could often believe it was a human voice. His magic tones are the most delightful heard since Paganini was here."

La Gazette des Theatres: "We can only repeat the praise which descends on him from everywhere for his powerful and brilliant technique, the purity and the wonderful precision of his staccato. His playing is that of a genius. Only an inspired artist blessed by God can coax such harmonic and soulful tones from his instrument."

Of all the endorsements, the review by the respected Jules Janin from the *Journal des Debats* was perhaps the most significant: "There are many tears and so much melancholy in his noble instrument, so much energy and power as well as grace under his iron bow! He is a musician who has not had a famous teacher and belongs to no school. There is something naïve, something inspired, with an incredible power."

Bull appealed to all strata of society; he was a particular attraction to women. Yet, amid the glowing reviews, financial rewards and the fervor of audiences wherever he went, the moody and temperamental Bull wrote of his despair in a letter sent to his mother in Bergen in December 1835:

At last, after a year's silence I will let you know that I am still alive . . . alive—oh! My torments and tribulations, my soul's restlessness and the thousand times repeated death pains in my broken heart unhappily remind me that I am alive. Alas, how dearly bought is the spark of Prometheus!!! I strove for a name that will survive me. I have attained it. Alas! I did not see the thorns that convulsively entwine my rose, which is ever more so encircled as to be strangled. I look ahead with courage to my end.

I can never become happy. Sufferings are my sustenance. I will give my anxious heart air. Loneliness is my friend, perhaps the only true one that I possess. It accompanies me in my throes of death, on the stage, amidst the applauding public, and sits beside me in my silent chamber at this moment.

It is now midnight. For three weeks I have hardly slept a single night. An inner voice confines me to my compositions until dawn, as if someone were asking me to hurry my labors while there is still time. My ideas arise so clearly to my searching glance that I am taken aback and astonished as if by something supernatural, incomprehensible . . . Oh mother, mother! You also have your sorrows. We will meet again some time. Farewell! Farewell! Don't forget your Ole.

It is unclear what factors prevented Bull from returning to Norway, or sailing for America. He had the financial means and the incentives, but perhaps his physical health, his affection for Felicie or his tendency to live for the day and wallow in self-pity offset his desire to travel back home or visit the New World.

Bull eventually purchased a huge carriage to transport him, along with a servant and his provisions, throughout Europe. He also took the daring step of performing nothing but his own compositions before certain audiences. His appearances were almost always sellouts during an exhaustive concert schedule. Vast sums of money were spent almost as quickly as he earned them.

A May 1836 review in the *London Times* described his extraordinary playing in some detail:

A more completely successful performance of this kind we have never attended. His varieties of movement seem almost unlimited, and much as Paganini has done, this artist has certainly opened a new field on that instrument. His style is essentially different and, like that of every true great master, is of his own formulation. Perhaps his most remarkable characteristic is the quiet and unpretentious manner in which he produces all his great effects. There was no trick, no violent gesture. It seemed so easy that, to those not acquainted with the mechanical difficulties he mastered, it was not easy to comprehend that anything extraordinary had been done.

In long arpeggio passages and others made up of rapid and minute divisions, his bow scarcely seemed to move on the strings; his hand, too, was almost motionless, yet our ear was charmed with a succession of distinct and sparkling notes, which kept the whole audience fixed in mute and almost breathless attention.

His command of the instrument, from the top to the bottom of the scale—and he has a scale of his own of three octaves on each string—is absolutely perfect; in passing from one extreme of it to the other, however rapidly, he never missed a note . . . His 'quartette,' in the ordinary mode of playing, would seem impossible; but he distinctly made out chords of three notes with the bow, and he produced a fourth with his finger.

Young Felicie was still on Ole's mind, as reflected in a series of letters he sent to her Paris home. She had blossomed into a woman of subtle beauty, her oval face and fine features complemented by large, dark eyes, reflecting her Spanish descent. Bull interrupted his concert tour to travel to Paris, where the 26-year-old Ole and Felicie, eight years his junior, were wed on July 19, 1836.

Devoted to her husband and still youthfully timid, Felicie traveled to London with him and remained there to study English and music appreciation after Ole set off for Ireland and Scotland. Often accompanied by the renowned Robert Nicolas Bochsa, an aging French harpist, Bull embarked on a tour that featured more than 200 concerts. He thrilled audiences with compositions such as "Homage to Scotland" and "Farewell to Ireland," weaving airs of those nations into his original works.

On one occasion, as Ole's concert schedule brought him near London, Felicie traveled by stagecoach to see him. While she may have been feeling neglected, Felicie remained loyal to her husband and accepted her role as a subordinate— not uncommon for women of the 19th century.

Bull's preoccupation with his health and his compulsion for sympathy are clearly seen in this letter to Felicie, mailed from Bath: "I fear I may never see you again. I feel so ill at heart and in my head, and often I have a strong trembling. My eyes are so tired and my breast is as if it were slashed by a knife . . . If my powers should not be equal to my will and I should succumb, remember you have been loved, yea more than loved by your Ole Bull."

That she had been "more than loved" became evident when Felicie wrote to inform Ole that he was to become a father. She returned to her grandmother's care in Paris. Just weeks before their first child was born, Ole wrote to Felicie from Scotland, suggesting that they acquire the family's Valestrand property on Osteroy Island as their future home:

If you should wish to live quietly in this lovely district, we could study agriculture. The climate is very mild, the woods are populated only by deer, rabbits and foxes. The lakes have excellent trout, and the sea will supply us with salmon. Secluded there in our pretty home with our child, what would we lack? But this is only an idea that ran through my head as I thought of our future marital happiness. We shall see. For my part, I am tired of traveling in this way. I expose my health so that at least it will destroy me if I do not put an end to it. I compose every day here whether I am in bed or not.

Ole Storm Felix Bull was born Sept. 15, 1837. His father arrived in Paris two weeks later to greet his first-born and spend time with Felicie. Also while in Paris, Bull crossed paths with Paganini and was gratified that the legendary musician greeted him so warmly and was familiar with his work. Paganini praised Bull's individuality of style and predicted a brilliant career. This validation of his music by the great Italian was important to Bull. The visit also rekindled his sense of rivalry.

In an attempt to surpass Paganini and establish his own identity, Ole continued to work intensively on altering the construction of the violin and the piano. Soon, Bull was back on the stage, touring Germany, Russia, Finland and Sweden. In St. Petersburg, Ole learned through a letter from his brother Edvard that their father had died in early 1838. The long-anticipated reunion of Johan Bull and his highly successful son would never take place.

Bull was saddened that his father had never heard him play in public. He wrote to Felicie: "A letter from my brother Edvard describes most touchingly my poor father's death! He says he spoke often of the anticipated delight of his dear Ole's return, after so many years of separation. He read all the poems and criticism, and knew that I was on my way home, with my dear Felicie. He constantly heard divine music that made him forget his sufferings. When dying, he spoke of me, and his face was beautiful to behold."

In mid-June, Bull played three concerts in Sweden, accompanied on one occasion in Stockholm by teenaged vocalist Johanna Maria Lind, whose fame as Jenny Lind years later would rival Bull's in America. King Carl Johan Bernadotte embraced Ole Bull as if he were a native son. Bull was later fond of relating that he informed the king in no uncertain terms than he was a Norwegian, not a Swede.

Ole, Felicie and their baby boy arrived to a warm reception at Christiania in July 1838. During his absence, he had overcome physical ailments, harsh criticism and a limited formal education to become a national hero. Norwegians were eager to hear him perform and Bull did not disappoint them. He blended classical standards with melodies he had learned as a youth— somber ancient ballads, bold dance tunes, melancholy herding and love songs, religious standards and simple folk ditties. Audiences who resented the dominance of the Swedish and Danish cultures reveled in this newfound emphasis on music that was exclusively theirs.

"The greatest marvel of all was that he brought Norway home to the Norsemen," Wergeland wrote. "Most people knew the folk-songs and dances, but were ashamed to admire them. Lifted by him into their confidence and love, these homely melodies suddenly began to gleam like stars, and the people came to feel that they too had jewels of their own."

Ole Bull was a wealthy man at this point of his career, even as he spent his considerable earnings on violins for which he had little need, on his debt-ridden friends and on gambling and social functions for which Bull paid the tab.

As warmly as he had been received in Christiania, Bull was welcomed as a triumphant hero in his native Bergen. The occasion was particularly joyful for his mother, whose burdens had grown over the years in raising other children while her first-born traveled the world. Of Ole Bull's return, the local newspaper wrote, "Everyone was eager to see the much admired man, who as a child wandered among us without anyone's suspecting how famous he would become."

Amid the revelry, Bull set out for a trip to Valestrand. His father, in keeping with Norwegian tradition, had willed the island home to him. His popular "The Mountains of Norway" was inspired by his experiences in returning to this summer retreat of his childhood.

Soon, Bull was off on a tour that would take him from one end of Europe to the other. In Copenhagen, Ole befriended Denmark's Hans Christian Andersen, who was on the verge of becoming one of the world's greatest writers of children's literature. Andersen wrote this to Bull soon after they met:

We have known each other only for some days, but there are characters who you do not need to know for a long time to become dear to one another . . . Thank you for all the poetry that streamed out of your violin. If they could be reproduced in words, we would get a delightful cycle of poems! Even before I met you, I felt a strange sympathy with your genius, and now that we have met face to face and have understood each other, this feeling has been elevated to friendship. It must please you to know that you have won over a soul. Therefore I tell you so, and I am not ashamed of it.

After settling his family with relatives in Copenhagen, Ole was off to Germany in early 1839. Louis Spohr, anxious to make amends, welcomed Bull with open arms. Not all of the reviews were glowing. In Germany, music critics believed that virtuosos should master the work of the famous German composers of the past before relying on their own works. Bull's audiences were seemingly unaffected by these observations, but Ole himself was offended.

While performing in Breslau, Bull received a letter from Felicie informing him that young Ole had died. Bull wrote back of his devastation and sorrow, adding, "I still hope, not for me. No, for you, for mother and family, for my fatherland, my Norway, of whose name I am proud."

Felicie rejoined her husband in Vienna and accompanied him for a time on his travels. Bull chose Vienna to unveil his rendering of the clarinet adagio in Mozart's "Quartette in D Flat, Transcribed for Violin." Occasionally Bull referred to Mozart as "my religion," considering him unrivalled in his expressions of human thought and aspiration.

At a Vienna performance on March 2, 1839, composer Robert Schumann sat quietly amid the audience, then wrote a letter of his observations to his fiancé:

Ole Bull gave another brilliant concert. He belongs to the very best and yet he is still a learner. In the most colossal skill and purity he is the equal of Paganini and far above Lipinsky. Mayseder is a child beside him, and yet a more perfect human being; Mayseder has understood and resolved his life task. Ole Bull is not yet at his goal and I fear may never get there. His gifts for composition are still quite primitive, but there are some flashing sparks in it. With his many harmonics he would, however, make his way into your heart, of that I am sure.

While he was away, Bull maintained a keen interest in the developments unfolding back in Norway. He had observed, most notably in Bergen, a restlessness and concern over worsening economic conditions and government intrusions. Two more ships, carrying 167 passengers, had left Stavanger in 1836. The following year, the *Enigheden* from Stavanger and the *Aegir* from Bergen sailed to America. An exodus from eastern Norway also began that year. Norwegians began to establish communities in the Illinois areas known as Fox River and Beaver Creek, as well as Rock County, Wisc.

Norwegians had also been following the experiences of Hans Barlien. A native of Trondheim, Norway's third largest city, Barlien had fought for social, religious, political and economic reform as a member of the first regular national legislature. His challenging attitude toward officialdom met with opposition and outright hostility.

Disillusioned and embittered, Barlien sailed for America in 1837, to found a colony for Norwegians who were dissatisfied with conditions in their home country. A number of Norwegians did join Barlien at his settlement at Sugar Creek, Iowa. Most, however, were attracted to the Mormon sect that developed in the colony and relocated to Mormon communities in Utah.

In a letter which was published in several Norwegian newspapers, Barlien wrote:

At last I can breathe freely. No one is here persecuted on account of his religious belief; anyone is permitted to worship God in his own way, as his conscience dictates. Pickpockets, lawyers, unscrupulous creditors, a corrupt government, and vagabonds have lost all power to harm people. Any occupation is free, and everyone reaps the fruits of his own industry. By wise legislation the Americans are safe against oppression. The so-called free constitution of Norway has so far only served to oppress the people with a continually increasing tax burden for the benefit of the governing class, and to foster luxury and laziness; such conditions must of necessity lead to general ruin.

Another publication sought to temper the enthusiasm of potential Norwegian emigrants. Entitled "Information on Conditions in North America," this 10-page pamphlet was authored by Sjur Jorgensen Haaeim, then published and widely promoted in Bergen by Bishop Jacob Neumann, a staunch opponent of emigration. Haaeim wrote of widespread disease, poverty and the absence of churches and schools in the U.S. He also warned of high taxes and the inability of farmers to support their families due to the expenses of land and machinery. Most remarkable is this passage, which foretells of Ole Bull's fate:

Oleana

Altogether too many are cheated when they come into the wilderness and settle on a piece of land, as everyone is entitled to do if he can pay the set price when the auction is held; but, if he is so unfortunate at that time as not to have enough money to pay for it in cash the same day, then any man who has money may buy the land . . . If he who has bought the land cares to compensate the occupant for improvements on the property, you can thank his generosity for that; if not, no one can make any legal claims on him.

Everyone ought to bear this in mind who intends to settle on such a piece of land; many of the Norwegians have worked several years, built houses, plowed the fields, built fences, and one thing or another, and have obliged to leave all without the least compensation. It often happened that the American people merely looked to their own interests, and in many affairs the Americans showed themselves utterly undependable; they were ready enough to promise but it was a rarity when they kept their promises.

The popular notion that Norwegians arrived in the U.S. ready and willing to be assimilated into American society is largely a myth. The truth is that many saw America primarily as a land of great economic opportunity. They intended to stay for a few years, make a considerable amount of money, and return to Norway to live the rest of their lives. However, to Ole Bull, the concept of emigration ran deeper. He began to see himself as a world emissary for the oppressed citizens of his native land. As he traveled across Europe, Bull was torn between obligations to his family and country, and his need to explore his own musical horizons.

While his own compositions formed the foundation for his concerts, Bull often played a Spohr or Paganini concerto, most often the crowd-pleasing "Carnival of Venice," based on the original Venetian air discovered by Paganini. Frequently he embellished "Carnival" with his own intricate imitations of birdcalls, street noises and the sound of lapping water.

Meanwhile, back in Copenhagen, Felicie was grief-stricken over the loss of their son and tired of the isolation she felt as her husband set a relentless pace abroad. Pregnant with the couple's second child, she longed to return to her grandmother's house in Paris. Bull arranged for his wife's return to France, joined her briefly in Paris, and then set off alone for more concerts in the Rhine basin. In November, he received from Felicie a letter announcing the birth of Alexander Ole Felix Etienne Bull. "He is your spitting image," she wrote, enclosing a lock of the infant's hair.

"My dear, think of my surprise and delight when I received the happy news!" he replied. "Let us praise God for his goodness to us, and let us hope that He will preserve our son to us."

Weeks later, from Frankfurt, Germany, he wrote:

Oh, if only you knew, Felicie, how it wearies me to belong to the world, and only for a few moments to myself, you would understand my distaste for it. I have to pull myself together if I am not to seem like a bear (and even then some find me bizarre and strange). In addition I feel the emptiness doubly. I see that all these annoyances are making me bitter and perhaps ungrateful towards fate, but is anything else possible?—Courage, courage! I shout to myself every moment of the day. My head is full of plans. There are so many people around me who fill my ears all at once that I don't know who I should listen to.

Ole returned to Paris to see his wife and newborn during the winter of 1839-40, working on compositions and performing occasional concerts. In March, plagued once again by financial worries, he embarked on a second English tour. He claimed that he was being cheated of money and otherwise exploited because of his generosity and trusting nature.

"I am persecuted on every side!" he wrote in one letter to Felicie, explaining how a business agent had defrauded him, forcing him to sue. When she expressed disappointment that Ole's concerts were not producing the promised riches, Bull defused the tension with words of affection, such as this letter sent May 15, 1840:

Your last letter has given me a moment of ecstasy, but also of sadness at not having you nearby to tell you how much I love you and how proud I am of belonging to you. In my life as an artist you have been my ideal, to whom I have directed my complaints, communicated my joys, babbled loving words. I have, so to speak, probed into your soul in order to become one with you. I have uttered reproaches as to no one beside my own self, thereby I have honored you above all other fellow beings . . . In reality, we are two hotheads— such as only the most exalted and devoted love can create.

In London, Bull was introduced to Franz Liszt, who had dazzled audiences in many European cities with his piano virtuosity. Bull and Liszt, similar in age, physical stature and theatrics on stage, appeared together for a concert series of legendary proportions in London, then in Germany.

"Liszt's head tossing and his expressive hands rising to exaggerated heights over the keyboard, Ole's caressing of his violin and his look of seraphic rapture— these affectations delighted their audiences, for people in those days reveled in public barings of the soul," wrote biographer Mortimer Smith.

Bull acknowledged that he and Liszt were "inspired with admiration and sympathy for each other." However, the two parted company on the serious issues of music composition. Whereas Liszt was meticulous in his attention to detail, he was appalled at the haphazard way in which Bull tended to his own manuscripts. Bull made light of Liszt's persistent chiding. Had he heeded Liszt's advice, the world would have a much better record of Bull's unique musical creations.

It seems that Bull was his own harshest critic and may have hidden some of his greatest works, as evidenced by this letter he sent to Felicie a few weeks before meeting Liszt: "I have still much to do as regards my compositions themselves, and my playing of them, before they are satisfactory to me. I find every day that there are improvements possible, and grave errors to be corrected, but I have a firm will, and am trying to do better and better. It is very fortunate that none of my compositions are published; I shall take good care not to have this done for some time."

"He left nothing, save the memory of his playing," biographer Smith lamented. "Hardly any of his compositions suggest the qualities of the man or make clear his hold over audiences; his more elaborate pieces need the highly individual interpretation of their creator to have much meaning for modern audiences. It is only in his simple tuneful melodies that we are able to catch a fleeting glimpse of the poet that was in him . . . the sad, sweet humanity of the minstrel who touched the hearts of people everywhere."

The family reunited in 1841, traveling to Bergen and on to Valestrand. They remained on the island for several months, experiencing the joy of their third child's birth. A son, Thorvald Bull, arrived on Aug. 17.

Audiences were clamoring for Bull to return, particularly in the Norwegian capital. Despite his wife protestations, Ole yielded to the temptation and departed for Christiania. While the Valestrand home provided most of the essentials, Felicie felt out of place on the island, depressed and disillusioned as she tended to young Alexander and Thorvald.

"The weather is horrible; it is the worst climate I have ever seen," she wrote. "It is so sad here. The loneliness is frightful, but I must live for my children, who some day will love me, I hope."

Bull was too immersed in his career, his causes and his own indulgences to rescue his wife from her drudgery. So emphatic were the audiences that critic Andreas Munch wrote, "He is no longer playing here and I think that is for the best. He has confounded our heads and emptied our purses. His playing exerts a magic that overwhelms our intelligence and throws all misgivings overboard. It is impermissible to play so beautifully."

From Amsterdam, he explained to his wife why he felt compelled to continue his musical career at the expense of his family and all else:

"Art is ever dearly bought, and the true artist easily deceived, for it is only by renouncing the material good that he may obtain the divine happiness of following the guidance of his imagination and creative power. To understand himself rightly, he must renounce all else, give himself wholly to his art, and fight ignorance and stupidity. I am not the man to give up the battle!"

That Bull chose during his early adulthood to "give wholly to his art" was one of the tragedies of his life, wrote his widow, Sara Bull:

He made no attempt to order his business in detail, but left to others what he could have readily mastered, always waiting for results to justify the enterprise; and this dependence was an unfortunate habit for a generous, sensitive, trustful man . . . He was not suspicious by nature, and lent too ready an ear to the suggestions or pretensions of others; his sympathetic nature and his needs making him an easy victim for designing persons and giving rise to his chief troubles.

Curiously enough, those who had grossly betrayed his confidence often found that they could not do without the charm of his presence after once having known it, however they might disregard his interests and happiness; and they knew that he could not but be generous to a vanquished foe. He used to say, "I will not, because one man has failed me, expect the like of another, until it comes." His trust in the good impulses of human nature never failed him long. Leaving home at the age of seventeen, wholly untrained in practical affairs, he worked out many a problem of life, as of art, at the hardest— through bitter experience in poverty and tears; but the ideals and aspirations of his youth were those of his age.

Ole returned to Norway in July 1842, spending a month with Felicie and children at Valestrand before moving the family to a home in Christiania. This arrangement did not last for long. When Ole departed on his next tour, Felicie returned to Paris to continue raising their two sons in an atmosphere where she felt more comfortable.

THE OLE BULL COLONY

Restlessness and a defiant national pride, punctuated by rebelliousness, marked the next stage of Ole Bull's life. He was constantly seeking stiffer challenges and new adventures. In Stockholm, Sweden, he found himself at odds with the Royal Orchestra. Exaggerated accounts of Bull's denunciation of the orchestra, the royal family and Swedes in general so offended the musicians that they refused to perform with him. Henrik Wergeland, livid that his fellow artist faced such treatment, published a biographical work on Bull in an effort to set the record straight.

A daughter, Eleonore Genevieve Felicie, arrived in May 1843, but even this failed to curb his wanderlust. When he wasn't performing, he was composing— perhaps taking to heart the advice of Franz Liszt. Bull committed to paper in early 1843 at least three compositions, including his "Adagio Religioso."

Inspired by the successes of other musical greats, he resolved to try his own fortune in America. His trip was motivated as much by curiosity and dreams of riches as by his frustrations over criticisms of his work. From Copenhagen, he sent Felicie a letter detailing his plans. "I am preparing by writing letters and advertising, for without that and great endurance, courage and strength, it is impossible to make one's way there, even with the greatest of talent."

Felicie protested: "I have never been so sad and unhappy as I am now, and I see the future in the darkest light! You are leaving for America and are happy, for you know that you will be taken care of, flattered and feted everywhere, but you do not think of the fact that we may never see each other again."

Ole assured her this tour would eliminate their financial worries once and for all and, upon his return, he would settle down and attend to his family's needs. He celebrated his impending departure by climbing through rain, sleet and snow to the summit of Snohetta, a mountain in the Dovre range then thought to be the highest in Norway, to play a farewell song on his violin.

Four

Accompanied by business manager Julius Schuberth, a young Norwegian secretary and a German valet, Ole Bull boarded the Royal Mail steamship *Caledonia* on Nov. 4, 1843, at Liverpool, England. He was bound for an America that was starving for cultural enrichment. However, if he thought that his going to the U.S. would free him from rivalries and criticism, he was badly mistaken.

Some of the Belgian and French musicians who preceded Bull to New York sought to discredit him, a situation that gave fodder to American newspaper reporters. Ole quieted his critics and bested his rivals with his most formidable weapon: the violin. His debut of Nov. 25, 1843, was reported in the *New York Herald*:

We cannot describe Ole Bull's playing— it is beyond the power of language. Its effects on others may be indicated. Some of his unearthly—his heavenly—passages work on the feelings and the heart 'til the very tears flow. Others it makes vociferous, mad, and terrible in their applauses. At the close of some of his wonderful cadences, the very musicians in the orchestra flung down their instruments and stamped and applauded like madmen.

This extraordinary being—this Ole Bull—will produce an excitement throughout the republic unlike anything that ever took place in our day. He is young, tall and elegantly formed, as beautiful as Apollo, with an affectionate simplicity of manner that wins all hearts and all souls. He is the most extraordinary being, the most perfect genius in his art that ever yet crossed the great Atlantic, and rose upon the bright horizon of the new world.

Six concerts in New York were followed by performances in Philadelphia, Baltimore, Washington and Richmond, all of them earning lavish praise that reinforced Bull's reputation as the best violinist of his day. His strong physique, simple diet and exercise regimen provided Bull with the necessary endurance. Traveling by railroad, stagecoach, canal barge and steamboat, he went on to perform in almost every major U.S. city east of the Mississippi River. In some venues, an orchestra was engaged to accompany him, but on many occasions he had only piano accompaniment.

He reported to Felicie that he had earned upwards of 40,000 francs deposited with his banker in Amsterdam. Her terse response informed Ole that she was expecting another child.

Bull thrilled audiences wherever he performed. One of his most fervent supporters was Lydia Maria Child, an American writer, poet and intellectual, who greatly admired him. She wrote in the *Boston Courier*:

They tell me his performance is wonderfully skillful; but I have not enough of scientific knowledge to judge of the difficulties he overcomes. I can readily believe of him, what Bettina says of Beethoven, that "his spirit creates the inconceivable, and his fingers perform the impossible." He played on four strings at once, and produced the rich harmony of four instruments. His bow touched the strings as if in sport, and brought forth light leaps of sound, with electric rapidity, yet clear in their distinctness. He made his violin sing with flute-like voice, and accompany itself with a guitar, which came with ever and anon like big drops of musical rain.

How he did it, I know as little as I know how the sun shines, or the spring brings forth its blossoms. I only know that music came from his soul into mine, and carried it upward to worship with the angels . . . While I listened, music was to my soul what the atmosphere is to my body; it was the breath of my inward life. I felt more deeply than ever that music is the highest symbol of the infinite and holy. I heard it moan plaintively over the discords of society, and the dimmed beauty of humanity. It filled me with inexpressible longing to see man at one with Nature and with God; and it thrilled me with joyful prophecy that the hope would pass into glorious fulfillment.

America surpassed all of Bull's expectations. His letters to Felicie told of his wonder as he observed railroads, growing cities, colorful steamboats and a variety of religious sects. Offstage, life was not so harmonious. A flap with Schuberth over the arrangements for a concert in Baltimore led to the business manager's dismissal. Schuberth promptly filed suit for breach of contract. The matter remained unresolved as Bull continued his concert tour.

First was a brief engagement in New Orleans in January 1844, where Bull was disappointed by audience reaction to his music and what he described as "jealousy and rivalry" from other musicians. "How do I like New Orleans? Not a great deal," Bull told one interviewer. "The people here prefer the nigger's violin to mine. I have traveled from New York to play to people who do not understand me."

Next was a seven-week trip to Cuba, where Bull composed two pieces based on local themes, "Cuban Potpourri" and "Memories of Havana." He wrote of his enthusiasm for what he described as a "fairy-like" atmosphere and the islanders' sincere appreciation of his music.

Felicie's patience was wearing thin, as she tended to the needs of their growing family. She professed her love for Ole, but let it be known in her letters that she was anxious for his return to Paris. Bull, immersed in his career and enthralled by America, offered little hope for an imminent reunion.

"I shall work for you and our children, and do all in my power to assure them a good education," Bull wrote. "This is a great and sacred duty." He seemed almost defiant in defending his trip to the New World. Bull was interested not only in music, but also in politics, social justice and economic advances in a rapidly expanding civilization. Of particular concern to him were the difficulties that newcomers were encountering.

Higher-than-expected travel expenses had hindered many Norwegians, prohibiting them from buying land on which to support themselves by farming. Food and work were hard to come by. Some suffered illness due to cramped quarters on the voyage over, combined with the cool, damp climate, different drinking water and changes in diet. Typhoid fever and dysentery were chronic on some of the immigrant ships. Fever, malaria and cholera were also common among immigrant populations.

May 1844 found Ole Bull in Boston for a much-anticipated series of five concerts. One guest at Bull's first Boston performance, poet Henry Wadsworth Longfellow, was particularly impressed by the famous Norwegian and sought out his company. The two became friends and spent many hours together at Longfellow's Cambridge residence, Craigie House, a beautiful home that has since become a museum.

While in Boston, Bull carried his violin into hospitals and mental institutions, much to patients' delight. He traveled to French Quebec and then to New York City, where the society crowd embraced him. Bull spent time with Edgar Allen Poe, Horace Greeley and Catherine Sedgwick, as well as others from the elite literary and social circles.

There are many subtle and overt references to Bull's appeal to the opposite sex. Of his stay in Boston, biographer Mortimer Smith wrote: "Such a figure was bound to flutter the hearts of the highly impressionable ladies of the town; true genius, and in such handsome guise, rarely appeared in the humdrum life of the city, and there was a feminine rush to find places at his feet. These emotionally excited ladies deluged Bull."

The deep religious divisions between Protestants and Catholics in the United States intrigued Bull, who was not one to make public pronouncements of his spiritual beliefs. "There are more than a hundred different sects and religions, some of them very strange," he wrote. "The Unitarians are without doubt the best of them. They are characterized by good behavior, tolerance, and their simple doctrines: they believe in only one God, not in the Son and the Holy Spirit."

Inspired by his new acquaintances and his observations of the American vitality, Bull channeled his energies into musical composition. A weeklong stay at Niagara Falls produced his "Niagara," said to reflect his impressions of the roaring waterfalls in many varieties of light. On one moonlit evening, a raging forest fire added a blaze and silvery shimmer to the cascading water.

His "Prairie Solitude" centered on the descriptions he had heard of the American prairie land. He also produced "David's Psalm," a religious composition, and "To the Memory of Washington." The latter incorporated sounds of a battle, a march, alternate airs of "America" and "Yankee Doodle," as well as other patriotic effects.

"My homage to the memory of Washington is not mine alone," Bull explained. "It is the homage of the whole Norse folk that is heard through me. The principles for which this people drew the sword and shed their blood inspired the Norwegians, and strengthened them in their struggle for independence. The admiration of the Norsemen for American institutions and for their great founder was early implanted in my breast, and admiration for Washington and love of liberty were indelibly impressed upon the tablets of my heart."

Bull was between performances at a resort on Narragansett Bay, south of Providence, in June 1844 when he got news of the birth of another son, Ernest Bornemann Bull, who died only a few months later. He continued to send money to Felicie, even as he promised her more. "If only I had been able to gain some sound judgment beside my musical skills. But alas! I have too much neglected money matters, since I was ignorant of the true value of money. This must change— let us hope for the best. I shall persevere."

Bull's letters to Felicie reflected pride in his newest compositions.

However, American music critics—while respectful of Bull's performing skills—were not inclined to issue the unreserved critical acclaim he may have expected. His harshest critic was George Templeton Strong:

He is a great player, undoubtedly, but that he's no composer one may see by his orchestral parts, of which one can judge better than the solos. They are thin and miserable beyond expression, mere noise, perfectly trivial, and utterly without musical ideas. His theory of the sublime in music would seem to be that it rests on a happy combination of brass and kettledrums . . . He'll have his joke about all this when he gets home, and he'll probably give a series of comic lectures on American characters, illustrated with specimens of these performances and extracts from the newspaper criticisms and eulogies.

He went on to perform in Philadelphia, Louisville, Wilmington and then gave five concerts in New Orleans. What Bull declared as his "farewell concert" took place in New York on Oct. 30, 1845, before the grand master of the Masonic Lodge and many of its members, attired in full regalia. Bull gave proceeds to a fund for the widows and orphans of Masons.

In a letter mailed to Felicie as he prepared for his return to Europe, Ole wrote, "I hope that my long absence and the success and sympathy I have had in America will have an effect in Europe, even in France. My social standing has been greatly enhanced by association with the most distinguished and remarkable men and women here. My relationship with the Americans is that of an adopted child."

The American tour saw Bull travel more than 100,000 miles, giving upwards of 200 concerts in every city of importance. He contributed more than $20,000 to charitable institutions and $15,000 to accompanying musicians. The *New York Herald* said of his visits: "The unparalleled enthusiasm awakened by him everywhere and his popularity in every city were most remarkable . . . No artist has ever visited our country and received so many honors. Poems by the hundreds have been written to him; gold vases, jewels, etc., have been presented to him by various corporations. His whole remarkable appearance in this country is really unexampled in glory and fame."

Perhaps the best indication of Bull's own perspective on his first voyage to America can be found in this passage from Sara Bull's book, *Ole Bull: A Memoir* (Houghton Mifflin Company, New York, N.Y., 1882):

His belief in the sturdy common people of his own country and his love of freedom made him anticipate with great interest an acquaintance with a people who governed for themselves, and this acquaintance resulted in giving him greater hopes for his own land, which he proudly felt was able to show already the most liberal constitution of all the European monarchial governments.

He was then and ever zealous to the utmost, that every precedent which had been favorable to the growing power of the Norse people, through their constitution, should be jealously guarded. He insisted that their only safety and good lay in a demand for a fuller sovereignty of the people, and in their better education for such power.

To him, therefore, the interest of his first visit and sojourn in the American Republic was not confined to his profession. He was from the first, and to the last, an earnest student of republican government and institutions.

On Dec. 3, 1845, Bull boarded the *Baltimore* in New York for the voyage to France and reconciliation with Felicie and their children. A two-month stay with his family in Paris over Christmas gave Bull a chance to get better acquainted with Eleonore Felicie, who was only a few months old when he left for the U.S., as well as sons Alexander, 6, and Thorvald, 4. Bull was persuaded to perform on several occasions in Paris, only to find that the critics disapproved of his showmanship. Some even used the dreaded term, "charlatan." Typical of their reports was this critique by influential musician and writer Henri Blanchard:

There is more of the bizarre than of originality in his caprices; and because these caprices have seduced the Yankees of the United States and have earned a great number of dollars because of the naïve admiration of these estimable merchants of the other world, is no reason why they should have the same result in this country, where good taste, elegance, style and nobility are the primary elements of all the arts.

One might apply to the Norwegian virtuoso this petty epigram which we are sure will not anger him because to understand the joke one must be French: 'Monsieur Bull has a great deal of talent, but . . . but, but, but, but, but . . . the buts will never be finished.'

At about this same time, his younger brother Knud Geelmuyden Bull (1811-1889), a talented artist, was being sentenced to 14 years of hard labor for having printed counterfeit Norwegian notes in London. He was sent with hundreds of other British prisoners to Norfolk Island in the Pacific Ocean, a detainment facility known for its brutality. Knud Bull, who had studied painting in Germany under the noted Johan Dahl, became known for his romantic landscapes, suffused with atmospheric light and subtle coloring. Ole stayed in contact with his brother in their later years but could not persuade Knud to return to Norway or join him in the U.S.

While in Marseilles, Bull once again crossed paths with Hans Christian Andersen who by then had published a significant work, titled an "Episode in Ole Bull's Life," depicting Bull as a fairy prince.

Still stinging from the French critics' columns, an embittered Ole Bull opted to continue his career before friendlier audiences. Over Felicie's protestations, the magnetic pull of the stage lured Bull away from his family once again— but not before his wife was expecting another child. Ole sailed to Algiers, and then set off for a yearlong stay in Spain. The Spaniards' music, their fiery temperament and colorful personalities appealed to Bull. And the Spanish audiences appreciated his music, as well as his performing style.

The fact is that Bull, by nature, was not cut out for domestic life. "It is always necessary that you must travel so you can hear the 'bravos'," his wife wrote. When Felicie complained of his lavish spending habits and neglect of their children, Ole claimed to be cruelly misunderstood. "Unhappily we do not understand one another— we both suffer under it."

Late in 1847, Bull returned to France, reconciling with his wife and planning an ambitious concert schedule. The February Revolution of 1848 awakened the hopes for national liberation in many European peoples. To Bull, it was an opportunity to demonstrate on behalf of his own country. He joined other Norwegians in Paris in a congratulatory address to the prime minister and leader of the February revolution, the poet Alphonse Lamartine.

Felicie and the children moved from Paris to the home of her relatives in Saint Michel, a small town on the Meuse River in northeast France. Bull traveled back and forth from a Paris hotel room to Saint Michel, providing him his first opportunity to get to know his new daughter, Lucie Edvardine, born in 1846. Much of his time in Paris was spent with an old friend and violin builder, Jean-Baptiste Vuillaume, as he continued to experiment with structure changes that could produce subtle differences in his instruments' tone or capabilities.

Late in 1848, he purchased the Norwegian island of Andoen (now Andoya) on the south coast near the town of Christiansand. Felicie expressed her concerns: "I wonder at your delight over Andoen, a property you don't know. It seems to me that you should have looked at it before you bought it." Nevertheless, she agreed to move there, in the hopes that Ole would be encouraged to spend more time with his family.

The developments in Paris sparked a sense of patriotism in Ole Bull that he hoped to instill in his native people. After a five-year absence from his homeland, he poured himself into a project aimed at awakening the national spirit in the capital city. Young Norwegian artists angered by the government's refusal to lend support to the emerging native art found a natural leader in their returning hero, who was at the peak of his creative powers and energy. A national art festival in Christiania called attention to their cause.

Bull's rendering of his new composition, "A Visit to the Saeter," became a national sensation. Its popularity can be traced to not only its combination of uniquely Norwegian folk melodies, but also the original melody, "The Dairymaid's Sunday," sometimes referred to as "The Herd Girl's Sunday." An accompanying poem by Jorgen Moe written after Bull composed the piece captures the melancholy feelings of a young shepherdess as she hears the church bells and thinks of her fiancé far away. It remains Bull's most popular and enduring composition.

After visiting Felicie and the children at Andoen, Ole was bound for Bergen. Inspired by the success of the art festival, he began plotting an even more ambitious project to preserve the uniquely Norwegian cultural traditions in his hometown. Bull found a natural ally in painter Fritz Jensen. Together, they devised a plan to develop a "Norwegian Theater at Bergen," free of Danish or Swedish influence. Only Norwegians would be eligible for employment as writers, actors or musical accompanists.

Jensen was designated as the theater director and Bull's brother Edvard, a music teacher with some conducting experience, was named orchestra director. But it was the involvement of Ole Bull that piqued the interest of the masses. In response to a newspaper advertisement seeking actors, musicians and dancers, townspeople turned out in droves, anxious to support their native son and share in his success.

Most of the applicants possessed little artistic talent. Jensen did finally assemble a troupe of nine actors and actresses. Among them was 17-year-old Johannes Brun, who would later become a famous comedian.

Edvard Bull, facing the same limitations in talent that frustrated Jensen, was able to blend musicians of modest ability with a handful of accomplished performers. Through private lessons and exhaustive rehearsals he molded an ensemble of which he was proud.

The building itself was a 50-year-old abandoned theater, unheated, and in need of major repairs. Contracted laborers and volunteers refurbished the structure while Bull continued his promotional work. He performed benefit concerts and made speeches calling upon Norwegians to join him in preserving and promoting their unique musical and dramatic traditions.

About 400 people were invited to a Nov. 21, 1849, rehearsal for the theater's first performance, the musical comedy entitled "Henrik and Pernille." They were impressed with the talents of Brun and the quality of the performance, highlighted by selections from Mozart's "Jupiter Symphony" and a rousing rendition of selections from Bull's own "A Visit to the Saeter."

Twenty public performances were scheduled for early 1850 and tickets were quickly sold out as momentum continued to build. Bull could not contain his own zeal, as reflected in this letter to Felicie:

Finally the great day has come which shall cast its light upon our national theater! Last week I tried it out on the public and invited representatives of the theater and some others to attend a rehearsal. The result was overwhelming! The audiences themselves declared that they were not only enthusiastic, but convinced that here were talents of such a remarkable kind that they had never seen their equal in Bergen.

Ah, Felicie— I would give a great deal if you could have been there; for you would have understood the relief that I felt at the first rehearsal. I would like so much to come as often as possible to see you and how you and our dear children are, but unhappily I cannot now. It is necessary for the national honor to carry out this work— and the work will go on; it is a national monument! I embrace you lovingly.

Felicie did not share her husband's enthusiasm. From the Andoen island home, she wrote: "The stay here is not very pleasant. The weather is terrible; there is a constant storm, and at night one can't sleep for the howling of the wind, and the house is only a summer structure . . . 'Poor mother!' you write. 'She's weeping.' I'm also weeping— but there is no one who hears or pities me."

In his reply, Ole wrote, "I wish you much happiness, health, satisfaction and PATIENCE."

Felicie wrote back, congratulating her husband on the success of his theater and regretting that she was not there so "at least I could enjoy your triumphs. But is after all not my lot to have many joys in life."

Bull saw no limit to the Norwegian Theater's potential. However, crowds were less than enthralled with the native offerings of the obscure Norwegian folk musicians. They sometimes chatted during the shows and treated the performers more as curiosities than as legitimate artists.

At the same time, a series of conflicts developed between Ole Bull and the Bergen Police. Accustomed to supervising public events and having their own way, the police demanded that several seats in the coveted orchestra section of the Norwegian Theater be reserved for their use. Bull eventually capitulated, but only after arranging for the utter humiliation of the officers. He mounted a sign over a section of undesirable seats in the back, reading, "These seats are reserved for the police." The audience entered into the spirit of the jest and laughed heartily at the officers and their guests. Bull and others were taken to the police station for booking.

These actions created a public uproar pitting those who sided with Bull against those who supported the police. Officers began following Ole Bull wherever he went. Soon, he was arrested for smoking a cigar on the wharf, based on an obscure law dating back to the Hanseatic days. What should have been a minor episode took on a whole new dimension when Bull refused to pay his fine and insisted on a public trial. This was the perfect opportunity for the mischievous Ole Bull to rally townspeople against an officious police force.

By coincidence, a hearing was held on Feb. 5, Bull's birthday. Revelers descended on the courthouse to show their support for Bull and their contempt for the police, prompting the authorities to drop the charges.

This feud grew more intense and widely-publicized after Bull was formally arrested for the incident at the theater, on a charge of "frivolous mockery of the august persons of the police." He appealed to the Supreme Court of Norway in Christiania, where his lawyer, the prominent Bernhard Dunker (1809-1870), who was also a friend of Bull's, successfully argued that granting of the seats was a courtesy, rather than a legal obligation. The attorney's sarcasm and ridicule of the complaining officials might have been more effective if reported in the newspapers. However, not a paper in the kingdom dared to report the defeat of a government official.

The Bergen police continued to annoy Bull at every opportunity, although they were fighting a losing battle. There was no denying Ole's popularity, which extended to hundreds of children who took every occasion to torment his detractors.

These seemingly trivial disputes were of great significance to Bull, his son Alexander confirmed many years later. In a letter to his wife, Bull himself described it in these terms: "There are so many affairs and torments that it is a miracle I don't sink to the bottom. But as long as I can, I will work to my last drop of blood for the divine principle of freedom."

The theater's first season came to a close in April 1851, at which time Bull purchased the theater outright from the Dramatic Society. The sale was conditional upon the theater being used exclusively for the performances of Norwegian artists.

With a ceremonious sendoff, Ole set out on a concert series to support the theater. Meanwhile, a second season opened in October with consistently large audiences. Following performances in Christiania, Denmark and Germany, Bull returned to Andoen in early 1851 and was surprised to find that Felicie and children had moved to Christiania.

To Ole Bull, the ultimate success of the Norwegian Theater hinged on an annual allotment from the Norwegian Parliament. However, Norway's elected officials were conservative in nature, representing an established order, and were not willing to sanction an institution that, in the eyes of the more puritanical members, was sinful and unnecessary.

"If one cannot maintain the nationality and the language in other ways, they will have to go by the board," declared Soren Jaabaek, the leader of the Agrarian Opposition, a liberal political party comprised of farmers and other rural residents. "That Ole Bull has made the name of Norway known throughout the world could not be a reason to pay him, as it were, for it." Jaabaek's counterparts in the Parliament, the urban representatives, saw Bull as too much of a radical or irresponsible dreamer to support his request.

Bull perceived this rejection as the ultimate betrayal. It deepened his resentment of the establishment and lessened his nationalistic fervor. It was as if the vote was a dismissal of Bull himself and all that he symbolized. He spoke of leaving Norway permanently and assisting Norwegian emigrants in their efforts to settle in the New World.

"He became faint-hearted and lost his faith in the government—even the country," said A. O. Vinje, one of the Norwegian nationalist rebels in Christiania. "A man with his temper had to handle it as he did. I was so lucky to see him almost every day in that period, and everything I and others with me excused the Storting (Parliament), he could not. He said, as the old Romans, 'Ungrateful country! You will not even hide my bones!' His plan matured as if he wanted to sacrifice the last penny in his pocket and the last drop of blood in his heart."

As word of the government's rejection spread, a group of supporters in Bergen organized a massive arts festival to raise money for the struggling Norwegian Theater. Among the leaders was 23-year-old Henrik Ibsen, an obscure poet who impressed Bull with his intensity, his eloquence and his strong devotion to Norwegian traditions. As the two grew better acquainted, Bull came to admire the youngster for his insight into human nature and social consciousness. Ibsen was hired as a playwright and stage manager. He went on to become one of the world's foremost poets and dramatists, basing his most famous character, Peer Gynt, on the personal characteristics and experiences of Ole Bull.

Ibsen's arrival was the opening Bull had needed. As biographer Mortimer Smith wrote:

"The success of the music festival and the continuance of public interest in the face of official indifference did not alter Ole Bull's growing determination to quit the management of the theater. That determination was born not only of his impatience with the petty annoyances and obstacles placed in his way, but also of an inherent restlessness that would have compelled him to move on to other things, no matter how great the success of the theater project. He was not a worker and a plodder and he was incapable of sustained interest in any formal, organized effort. He craved new experiences and entered into them with unreserved enthusiasm, but after the first flush of excitement they invariably began to bore him.

Newspapers in Norway, filled in the late 1840s with exaggerated tales of poverty and suffering by emigrants to the U.S., had more recently carried letters setting the record straight by the "Chicago Vossings." This correspondence society, a group of immigrants from Voss, east of Bergen, sought to paint a realistic picture of America to those who might wish to follow them. One of their letters, which numbered in the hundreds, is excerpted here:

Here it is not asked, what or who was your father, but the question is, what are you? Freedom is here an element which is drawn in, as it were, with mother milk, and seems as essential to every citizen of the United States as the air he breathes. It is part of his life, which cannot be compromised and surrendered, and which is cherished and defended as life itself. It is a national attribute, common to all. Herein lies the secret of the equality everywhere seen. It is an American political creed to be one people. This elevates the lowly and brings down the great.

It would be far from our purpose to rouse a spirit of discontent, but as American citizens who have tasted the joys of being free of the yoke which tyrants ever bear with them, and having in common with you the Norwegian temper, love of liberty, and warmth of heart, we would say to you who dwell amid Norway's mountains: Show yourselves worthy sons of the north. Stand as a man for your liberties. Let freedom and equality be your demands, truth and the right your reliance, and the God of justice will give you victory.

Deeply disappointed and disillusioned, Bull left Norway in November 1851, stopping to perform in Hamburg, Amsterdam and London before reaching Liverpool. By this time, Felicie had run out of patience and a letter from her lawyer informed Bull that she was seeking a divorce. In reality, Felicie was still dependent on Ole and still longed to be with him. She did not have the financial means to support herself, had no home of her own and was too ill to press for dissolution of the marriage.

The problems with his marriage, the bitterness over the lack of government support for his Norwegian Theater and the lingering resentment of authority epitomized by the dispute with the Bergen Police— it was more than Ole Bull could take. He needed a new beginning, a new challenge. The time had come to move forward with his plan to develop a colony for his countrymen in America: the land of opportunity for all that he held dear.

So, accompanied by an individual anonymously described in the ship's log as a "servant," he boarded the Royal Mail steamer *Asia* in Liverpool for a return visit to the United States. Ole Bull was determined to seek out a place where his people could work the land, live together in freedom, harmony and prosperity while celebrating their national heritage— a "New Norway."

Five

What was Ole Bull thinking as the *Asia* pushed itself through the cold January seas toward America? He was inquisitive about the New World, anxious to learn more about potential sites for his colony. He was also deeply interested in the American political system, while intent on using his wealth, stature, personal appeal and vision to help his countrymen preserve their cultural identity and improve their life's circumstances, even if it meant abandoning their native land.

He was also eager to renew acquaintances with the American civic and cultural leaders who had so warmly embraced him several years earlier. The fulfillment he derived from music was no longer enough to satisfy Bull as he entered midlife. Public attitudes toward his work were changing, as well. He had for 15 years been a major sensation, enjoying widespread praise while he awed audiences across Europe. But other musicians were on the horizon at the same time musical tastes were changing. More and more, audiences expected a strictness and classicism that Bull found too restrictive.

At 42, Bull was a man of great charisma, vaguely handsome with deep-set, dark eyes and a tall, commanding presence. Word of his return to America and his mission of founding a new home for his countrymen spread rapidly. It was, as Mortimer Smith described, "an idea of such vast and staggering proportions that the scheme for the theater paled into insignificance behind it, and the proper setting for such a grandiose idea was that illimitable country toward which he now once more set his face."

Bull had for too long suppressed his desires to become involved in politics, nationalism and economics.

"The determination to increase his scope had unfortunate effects on the artist, but it added immeasurably to the fascination of the man," Smith wrote. "He was a man of great insight, with ideas that were often sound and sometimes brilliant, and he had a remarkable talent for scenting out genius in others, but he was under the persistent delusion that he had a knack for guiding affairs and men."

Never was there a better example of this than in Ole Bull's development of a colony in the mountains of Pennsylvania. It was an adventure that left its mark on his soul for the rest of his days. His dream was one of a new beginning for Norwegian commoners who had wearied of their unending strife and powerlessness in the homeland. Wrapped around these practical ambitions were Bull's vague notions of political and economic justice; let others work out the details.

The *New York Times* in its Jan. 18, 1852, edition, noted, "The celebrated Ole Bull, the Norwegian violinist so much and universally admired on his first visit to this country in 1843-4, arrived on the *Asia* Friday night. He is, for the present, on a quiet visit to New York without any declared purpose to renew his American concerts, but we can scarcely believe that he will not favor us with another touch of his fine quality before returning to Norway."

Bull visited old friends and admirers, such as Anne Charlotte Lynch, a New York poet and author with a well-known literary salon, to reveal his plans for a Norwegian colony in America. He also spent time with Mr. and Mrs. John Hopper, whom he had met in 1843 through their mutual friendship with Lydia Maria Child. It's likely that Ole Bull and John Hopper discussed the colony plan at this time, since Hopper was soon to become an interested party.

Bull proceeded directly to Baltimore to meet with his attorney, who had written him of the favorable termination of the old suit with Schuberth over the latter's service as manager of Bull's 1843 U.S. tour. He was then summoned to renew acquaintances with the aging U.S. Senator and former presidential candidate, Henry Clay. Bull told of the encounter in Lexington, Ky., a quarter century later when interviewed by a *New York Herald* reporter:

Henry Clay was very sick and I was invited to visit him by a mutual friend. I accepted and proposed that I should take my violin and play for him. The idea was approved by my friend, who said that Henry Clay would no doubt be delighted. On arriving at the house I took up a position in a room adjoining the sick chamber and played in a low tone Clay's favorite melody, "The Last Rose of Summer."

His interest was immediately aroused and he asked if someone was playing in the street. As the tone raised, he said, "Ah, that must be Ole Bull; no one but him could play that air." When I had ended, the doors were thrown open and the great man came and embraced me. I felt a higher honor than if all sovereigns in the world had embraced me. When the incident became known I was requested to give a concert in Washington, and the request was signed by the Senators and Representatives and also by President Fillmore. (Bull's sequence of events was apparently incorrect in this rendition)

His reply, printed in *National Intelligencer* of Washington, on March 24, 1852, read:

Gentlemen: With gratitude and pride I acknowledge the communications you have done the honor to address to me. Loyal to my arts, I rejoice that it is thus signally distinguished in me, its faithful votary. To embrace the opportunity you offer is at once pleasure and duty. In accordance with your invitation, I shall therefore give a concert on Friday evening next, the 26th instant. I beg offer you, gentlemen, the assurance of my most sincere respect.

Your obedient servant, OLE BULL

His first performance was so well received that he had to give another. Of the former, the *Washington Telegraph* wrote:

Carusi's Saloon last night presented the most splendid array we ever saw within it. It was Bull, and filled with as rich an aggregation of broadcloth, silks, satins, jewelry, beauty, intelligence, and intellectuality as can in this republic be well compressed within the limits of a hall of its proportions.

Ole Bull was evidently inspired by the scene before him. We never before knew what could be done with that much-abused instrument, the violin. It laughs and weeps, exults and complains, speaks and sighs, rides the billowy ocean, encounters storms and shrieks in affright, ascends craggy mountains and shouts upon their summits, descends to shadowy vales, and reposes in their groves.

We look with wonder upon the instrument, and upon the hands that operate upon it with grace and agility beyond conception, and we feel the magic influence of the spell by which he leads us whithersoever he would go. But there is another influence operating upon every spectator: it is the presence of the man! Ole Bull appears to be less than forty years old. He is tall, not thin enough to be called slender, yet lightly and gracefully formed. His temperament is triple— a blending of the bilious, nervous and sanguine; his head is good, his forehead clear and full; his eye highly expressive of kindness, good sense, and intelligence; his face is exceedingly prepossessing in feature and expression; and every look, action, and word appears to indicate the lofty conception of a child of nature; a true poet, and a true artist.

Last night, in a little extempore speech, the poetry of his nature was aptly illustrated. Bowing profoundly to the torrent of applause that rewarded his effort, he retired from the stage without perceiving the splendid bouquet that has been thrown to him by a lady sitting near the President. He instantly returned and seized the prize, then walked a pace or two forward and, in the most easy, graceful and earnest manner, said, "In this (presenting his violin) there are tones—only tones—and they will die and be forgotten; but the memory of the pure spirit that has given me this (placing the bouquet next to his heart) shall live forever."

An appreciative Henry Clay eventually returned the favor by having delivered to Bull at his Pennsylvania colony horses and cattle bred from the finest stock of that era.

Bull had another reason to visit the nation's capital. He wanted to learn about the inducements and advantages offered to lure emigrants to go to the Western States, so that he might match or exceed them in a colony of his own once the suitable land was acquired. He spoke incessantly of his colonial scheme, especially during social gatherings with the city's elite at the home of Fanny and Charles Eames. Fanny Eames was another of the many women enamored by Ole Bull. She guided him around Washington and was by his side as Ole discussed his aspirations with prominent acquaintances such as Daniel Webster, Charles Sumner and Hamilton Fish.

Speculators and land agents who had heard of Bull's plans and knew of his financial resources sought him out. In April, he inspected some property in Virginia's Shenandoah Valley. However, Ole Bull's staunch opposition to slavery eliminated any slave-holding state from consideration. The American institution of slavery contradicted Norwegians' image of the U.S. as the land of natural freedom, equality and liberty.

Bull also heard tales of privations, illness and other hardships from his countrymen who settled in the south. He went out of his way to let it be known in Norway and the United States that there would be good land and good pay to be had in an American colony he intended to found and populate with his countrymen. He spoke of it during his tour of southern cities and his subsequent concert stops in New York, Boston and Montreal. Back in New York, he conferred about the colony plan with John Hopper, now his attorney and agent, then returned to Washington while Hopper began making investigations of his own.

Soon, Hopper had developed a relationship with John F. Cowan, a Pennsylvania attorney and land agent, and his associate, Joseph T. Bailey of Philadelphia. They detailed to John Hopper the northcentral Pennsylvania property of 11,144 acres, available at a cost of $10,388. Under their scheme, Bull would also be given the right to enter a company of buyers to obtain another 120,000 acres.

There was much to be said for the land. The price was reasonable, the terrain was mountainous—resembling portions of Norway—the valley land was fertile, and there was healthy air with no threat of cholera or other disease. There were also prospects of a rail line soon being built to connect this remote area to the commercial world, as well as the presumption of mineral riches beneath the ground.

Bull was summoned to Philadelphia to meet with Hopper, Cowan and Bailey. It's possible that Bull purchased the property sight unseen, beginning with a $15,000 payment to Cowan to secure the rights and pay incidental expenses. Lucius E. Bulkeley, a Wall Street attorney who represented Bull, assisted the group in the formation of a colonial development company, with Cowan as superintendent and business manager, Bailey treasurer, and Bull president.

Townspeople in Coudersport were abuzz in the summer of 1852 when the local newspaper, the *People's Journal*, reported that Ole Bull had purchased "120,000 acres" of forestland in the southern section of Potter County and intended to populate the land with thousands of citizens from his native Norway.

As far removed as this northcentral Pennsylvania region was from the population centers where world-renowned musicians performed, many had heard of the great Ole Bull. Some proclaimed that Potter County's time had surely arrived. Blessed with abundant natural resources, the region had unlimited potential for population growth and prosperity— at least according to its early leaders. In the *People's Journal*, the area's attributes were extolled in no uncertain terms:

We have always believed that when our county became accessible by means of railroads or canals, it would soon become thickly settled;

and now we have proof of it. Ole Bull has commenced a colony on Kettle Creek, which we have no doubt will go on increasing until every foot of land in the county is occupied by a settler. Why not? When can a man do any better?

We can raise more and better potatoes to the acre than can be raised on any other land in the nation; fifty bushels of oats to the acre is quite an ordinary crop; two and one-half tons of hay is probably medium; and forty bushels of corn to the acre is a common yield. As for sheep, we should like to see a county that can surpass ours in natural advantages for sheep growing.

Now, as the wild land in this county can be bought for two or three dollars per acre, and the first crop will pay for clearing, we can't for the life of us see what is to prevent a farmer, if industrious, from getting rich. It is asked what inducement we offer to men to settle here rather than go to Wisconsin or Iowa. We reply, the inducements are numerous; first, good health; second, better prices for everything we raise; third, our soil is quite as productive; fourth, our glorious springs of pure and delicious water are worth more to any man than the difference between the price of our land and the open prairies of the West.

There are many other reasons why people in search of land for homes should come to this county in preference for going West; but the above are sufficient for sensible men. This colony of Ole Bull's is very favorably located. It is on the turnpike leading from this place to Jersey Shore, on which a weekly stage is run. It is on the headwaters of Kettle Creek, one of the finest streams in the county. The numberless springs which form the stream, bursting out from every hillside, are more valuable than gold mines.

So we look upon a very large ascension to our population the coming season as quite probable. We confidently predict that Potter County will, in a few years, send the best butter, beef and mutton to the New York market that is found there; and that we shall send more of it than any other county in the state.

Ole Bull arrived in Coudersport on Sunday evening, Sept. 5, 1852, accompanied by Mr. and Mrs. John Hopper and by John F. Cowan, whose name would come to be cursed by many of those seeking a scapegoat for the demise of Bull's settlement. Their arrival was duly noted by the *People's Journal*:

Our quiet village became excited last Sunday when words said that the world famous Ole Bull had arrived in the city. Since we were not informed about this visit in advance, several of our inhabitants were suspicious of the rumor. But when we met John F. Cowan, Esq., from Williamsport, all doubt disappeared, and we realized how fortunate we were. But we became even more surprised when we learned that this knowledgeable man had bought 1,200 acres of land in this county from Mr. Cowan, which he planned to open up for other citizens.

Ole Bull's fame, genius and wealth will make it possible to settle as many of his native countrymen as he wants on this new-bought land. That is why we see this as the most important event happening in the county's history.

Bull and his party had ridden from New York City to Wellsville, N.Y., the closest rail outlet to Coudersport, on the New York & Erie Railroad. They headed south toward Coudersport by stagecoach on the mail and passenger route linking the two communities.

Two days later, a group of about 30 skilled laborers, primarily from Norway and Denmark, recruited by Bull in New York followed the same route to Coudersport. Among them were carpenters, masons and other workmen who were hired to begin building the colony. Their arrival was described by the *People's Journal*: "There arrived some thirty fine-looking, robust and determined appearing sons of Norway on their way to Ole Bull's new possessions. These are the vanguard of an army which is to follow them when these pioneers shall have prepared shelter for them."

Spending the night in Coudersport, the visitors were up the following morning, anxious to see for themselves the land on which they and others would build the "New Norway." While that was the name by which the colony's reputation was spreading throughout both Norway and the United States, Bull preferred the name "Oleana."

They traveled by horse and wagon down the Coudersport and Jersey Shore Turnpike, named for the communities at each end. This was the only road of any length in the region, blazed through the wilderness to connect these two developing centers of mid-19th century commerce.

In Bull's vision, the Pennsylvania colony would rapidly expand, becoming a haven for thousands of Norwegians who shared his sense of national pride while, at the same time, giving Bull himself a political base from which to exert his influence on a whole nation—or so he hoped. A Philadelphia newspaper reported:

It is just recently that the northern counties in Pennsylvania have caught the settlers' attention. While thousands of immigrants flocked west to the unfriendly country, this vast region has been empty and forgotten. Now, everybody is surprised of this hidden treasure.

Thousands of immigrants are approaching; colonies after colonies are settling. The most interesting event lately has been the Norwegian settlers in Potter County, directed by Ole Bull. As everybody knows, he is world famous because of his violin. Until now, he has only been known because of his music. He deserves to be better known.

As a man of several enterprises and handy craft, there are few like him. It is an honor for our state to have him and his country fellows within our borders. His settlement is by the wooden land, south of Potter County, close to the Susquehanna River's western branch.

It is Ole Bull's intention to split up the 200,000 acres of large land; sell it to his countrymen for retail price so everyone can become owner of his own land. Every town shall have its own church, and every district a school for English and moral upbringing.

The land that Ole Bull and his group entered upon in early September 1852 can best be described as untamed wilderness. It lay in the Kettle

Creek valley of the Allegheny Mountains, narrow at its northern end and gradually widening toward the south, with steep, rugged hills on either side. Magnificent stands of virgin timber—white pine, hemlock and hardwoods—covered the hillsides so thickly that the area became known as the "Black Forest." Scattered timber cutting had commenced in the region, as investors arrived to exploit the valuable native pine. Log homes dotting the narrow road connecting Coudersport with more populated areas to the south were practically the only signs of human encroachment.

Four decades earlier, a clearing had been made along the turnpike in a slanted valley that would become known as Carter Camp in Abbott Township. A packhorse trail that emerged from the clearing was widened into a wagon road. Just before Ole Bull and his colonists arrived at Carter Camp, a post office had been established there. John Cartee, the road contractor hired to build sections of the Coudersport and Jersey Shore Turnpike, had a camp located in the clearing that first became known as "Cartee Camp." The evolution to "Carter" can probably be attributed to different dialects and common usage.

Complementing the seemingly endless expanses of forest was a river system, considered a major asset for development. A tributary known as Little Kettle Creek rises in West Branch Township and flows south across Abbott Township and through the Carter Camp area into northern Stewardson Township. In Oleana, Little Kettle Creek is joined by the Germania Branch, forming Kettle Creek itself. The river flows southwest, adding tributaries over the next ten miles and eventually emptying into the West Branch of the Susquehanna River.

The decade that preceded Ole Bull's arrival saw Potter County's population double to more than 6,000, but most of the residents had settled in the county's northern sector. The 1850 census showed a population of 54 in Stewardson Township, divided among 11 families; Abbott Township didn't appear in the census, since it was not officially established until January 1852.

Tax records from Stewardson Township in 1849 paint a revealing picture. They show a lumber mill assessed to Vaux and Stewardson; 14 oxen owned by the Dodg brothers; a patent lever watch owned by Ezra Pritchard. John Ashcroft is identified on tax records as a hunter, while 15 other men were taxed for having "occupations, cows, oxens or improvements." Miles Thompson had opened a mill in an area that was known as Thompson's Mills at the time, site of the present-day village of Cross Fork. Thompson was the second sheriff of Potter County.

An eyewitness account of the scene that occurred upon Bull's arrival at his Pennsylvania colony appeared in New York's *Courier & Enquirer* in September 1852. Reporter Eli Bowen accompanied Bull and the Hoppers as they traveled to the colony to meet up with the workers who preceded them to the clearing at Cartee Camp. His report captures the celebratory spirit of the occasion:

The immigrants had arrived before us, and supposing that was the end of their journey, had prepared to pitch their tents and had raised their flag, which they had made before leaving New York. It was a beautiful device— the cross of Norway in the center surrounded by the stars and stripes of the United States. As soon as Ole Bull appeared in sight, the immigrants commenced the most enthusiastic cheering, which we answered by standing up in our wagons, waving our handkerchiefs and swinging our hats.

Ole Bull could not wait for the slow motion of the horses, but leaped from the wagon and ran to embrace them; such enthusiasm and manifestations of delight are seldom witnessed. After the first greetings were over, Mr. Bull addressed them, saying that after having spent many months in examining different sections of the United States, he at last found a place where his beloved Norwegians could have a home, where the climate was as beautiful as their own Norway, the soil capable of supplying their wants, and where they could enjoy liberty, protected by wise and wholesome laws which would guard to them every right and privilege, so long as they remained good citizens. With tears in their eyes, they answered him with shouts and embracing.

This clearing was, in fact, *not* their destination. The Norwegians were bound for a wider section of the valley a few miles south. The group enjoyed a lunch of cold meat and bread, harnessed their horses to the wagons and proceeded on to Oleana. (Unfortunately, the name has since been changed to "Oleona," probably for the same reason Cartee Camp became Carter Camp— dialect and common usage.) Most researchers believe Bull himself named the village that was the hubsite for his colony, based on his own first name and that of his mother, Anna.

The group arrived at Oleana by early evening and settled in for the night outside the only building in the valley, a small two-story cabin that provided lodging for turnpike travelers. Bull secured a room there. The next morning, the work of building the colony began in earnest. Bull rode off on horseback with one of his advisors to explore his property and decide which areas should be developed to accommodate the waves of settlers who would be arriving in the coming months.

Some of the carpenters began construction of a hotel. Other lots were designated—rather haphazardly—for a blacksmith shop, barn, storehouse and other community facilities. Land was to be surveyed and laid out into small farms, to be sold at low prices with long payment terms. Each town was to have its own church and schoolhouse.

While Bull was off exploring, several wagons loaded with food, stoves, tools and other provisions arrived at Oleana. A yoke of working oxen and a fat ox, to be slaughtered for meat, were also led down the turnpike by workers Bull had hired in Coudersport.

To Ole Bull, there was no limit to the potential the Kettle Creek valley held for his people. After a brief return to check on progress, Bull rode off again to select a site for his own home and survey the flatlands where workers could begin building log cabins. Following the winding Kettle Creek, he found a point where the waters divided into two forks, forming a natural island in the middle, and decided that the land in-between would be an ideal site for a garden, nursery and fruit tree orchard, with the bounty to be shared among the colonists. Other sites were tentatively designated for a sawmill, gristmill, cabinet-making shop and a leather tannery.

Near the end of the first day, workers felled a huge evergreen tree and stripped its branches to form a flagstaff. The topmost bows were left as an ornament and the tree was raised from the top of the cabin. John Hopper's wife hoisted the flag with the Norwegian cross superimposed on a background of the stars and stripes. As it rose to half-staff, the breeze stiffened it. Reporter Bowen recorded the scene:

As soon as it was elevated and fastened, a large flock of birds came and perched upon it and commenced signing in the gayest and most delightful manner. It appeared as though they were inspired by the scene and were giving utterance to their feelings of joy and welcome to the great Norwegian and his followers. Regarding it as a good omen, we all united in giving the birds a hearty round of applause.

It had been arranged that the new name by which the town was hereafter to be known was to be pronounced as soon as the flag had reached its proper elevation. The cords for raising the flag were now adjusted, and all waited to hear the chosen name.

The flag ascended slowly and gracefully to its place. A gentle breeze floated it proudly in mid-air and the name "Oleana" was given to the new home of the Norwegians. Thirty-one cheers—one for each state—were given, and three more for Ole Bull.

Workers had piled logs, brush and shavings in an open area near the inn for bonfires to be ignited as part of the christening ceremony that night. Following dinner, Bull retired to his room with his violin to decide on appropriate music and to prepare a speech. As nightfall arrived, the new citizens of Oleana gathered outside the structure to await their leader's emergence. A chair and lanterns were arranged on the upper balcony.

The scene that ensued was captured by Eli Bowen:

The bonfires were lighted in every direction, which made it as light as day all around the hotel, while the unbroken forests and lofty hills which made up the background appeared, in the dread gloom and magnificence with which they were clothed by contrast of light, to be solemn spirits of a bigoted and tyrannical age, who had held humanity in bondage during long centuries, come to take their last look at their former oppressions, and then to vanish before the light of Christianity and Liberty into darkness and desolation forever.

At half past nine, Ole Bull appeared on the balcony and the hills resounded with echoes from the loud shouts that went up to greet him; he appeared to be impressed with the greatness and solemnity of the occasion and, while he gracefully and modestly bowed his acknowledgements, the tears were choking his utterance. As soon as he could command his voice, he addressed his countrymen.

Bowen filed a lengthy report that he assured readers was a representation of the speech's substance. Given Bull's reputation as an accomplished orator who chose his words carefully, and his oft-stated reverence for the American system of government and history of freedom and independence, the reporter's version would appear to be fairly accurate; Bull may even have given the writer his notes.

Brothers of Norway! From the clime where the north wind has its home . . . we have come to find a home. When we were among our mountains and war was bringing want and famine among us, we heard there was a country in a milder clime where liberty dwelt and plenty reigned. Upon looking over our records, we found that our countrymen, under Thorfin, had discovered that land more than 800 years ago, but that they were met by the cruel and savage Indians, and had left no record of themselves. Excepting some tracks of their sad history engraved in the rocks at Fall River, and one temple which they had raised to God on an island at the south of Narraganset Bay, all other record of them had passed away.

But since then we learned other events had transpired, other adventurers had sought that shore, and one of the great nations of the earth had been successful in planting colonies there; that these colonies had grown and flourished; and that when the mother country had endeavored to impose tyrannical laws upon them, they had rebelled. Standing up boldly in the presence of mankind, they had declared before Almighty God that they were free and independent; that they had been successful and had established a government with a written constitution, based upon the principles of justice and the eternal rights of humanity; that they had spread over almost the entire continent and had become one of the leading nations of earth; and that there a home could be found for all who sought it, but the right to labor for ourselves would not be denied us; and that our inalienable rights of life, liberty and the pursuit of happiness would be secured to us.

Overjoyed by the light and hope which this news gave us, we have sought this country to be partakers of this liberty, to enjoy this freedom, and here in this beautiful valley we have selected our home. The resounding echoes of every tree you can cut will be heard in Mother Norway, and bring our brothers to us, and we will establish here a New Norway, consecrated to liberty, baptized in freedom and protected by the glorious flag of America.

How different is our reception from that which Thorfin and his followers received! No savage Indian startles us with his war whoop, but kind friends meet us on every side, taking us by the hand and giving us welcome to our new home. Brothers of Norway! We must not disappoint this confidence, but by lives of industry and honesty show to our new brothers that they have not misplaced their friendship. And now, to these gentlemen of New York and Pennsylvania who have so kindly assisted by their counsel and advice in this work, I return my most sincere and heartfelt thanks, and casting ourselves upon the goodness of our Heavenly Father, resting secure in his promise, let us go on in that daily performance of every duty, and He will bless us.

Shouts of joy and celebration followed the presentation. Ole Bull then raised his violin and performed a wide selection of music, ranging from war songs and hymns of liberty well known by the Norwegians, to classical standards. The entire gathering sang a favorite patriotic song of their time, "For Norway, Land of Heroes."

"No language can describe this music," Eli Bowen wrote. "The auditors, the attendant circumstances, and the occasion appeared to have given a new and unearthly inspiration to the great artist; he touched every cord of every heart in his audience. Such was the beginning of the new town of Oleana. May its progress be onward and upward, and long may its distinguished founder live to be a blessing to his countrymen and to enjoy the luxury of doing good."

Filled with enthusiasm, Ole Bull was soon bound for New York to greet the next wave of Scandinavian immigrants and to tell the world about his New Norway.

Six

Several weeks before the celebration at Oleana, a brig known as the *Incognito* set sail from Christiania with 130 Norwegian passengers aboard. For many of the emigrants, this voyage represented a once-in-a-lifetime opportunity to improve their condition, even as they bore the emotional burden of breaking ancestral ties. Relatively few Norwegian families had the means to afford such a trip, and many of those who did had emptied their life's savings— no one was allowed aboard the ship without passage paid and $300 U.S. in gold.

Brigs from that era had severe space and weight limits, unlike the luxurious and well-equipped steamers that would follow. Those bringing more of their belongings than they could carry aboard were required to pay exorbitant freight fees, prompting many to sell or give away their household goods. Most were left with only their clothing, books and limited personal items.

The captain, S. Christophersen, was also the owner of this copper-binded vessel built in Drammen, Norway, in 1849. Her maiden voyage carried 132 passengers from Christiania to New York in 1850. The *Incognito* then transported cargo to and from Jamaica. The ship had several shorter trips before its second voyage from Christiania to New York, with 138 passengers, in 1851.

On the beams was laid a deck of planks with hatchways down into the hold, where the baggage was stowed away on top of the cargo. Two rows of bunks of rough boards were built up, one above the other, for most of the ship's length. Between these open bunks were special berths reserved for passengers whose space demands were greater.

Light and ventilation were admitted through open hatchways and partly through skylights in the deck. During storms and rough seas, canvas was placed over the hatchways. If this continued for any length of time the air in the room below became foul. Oil lamps burning night and day exacerbated the problem.

Each passenger had to supply himself with bedding and food, consisting chiefly of smoked and salted meat, flatbread and casks of sour milk. The ship was stocked with potable water and provisions for sale, in case the passengers' food ran out during the voyage. A porridge pot was boiling all day long.

Edvardt Olsen told of the tears that were shed as his sister Gina, wife of Jens Jacobsen Skoien, and his other sister Sofie departed Christiania on July 6, 1852:

Jacobsen had been a farm foreman for some time and also a carriage driver. Gina had little desire to travel and persuaded her sister Sofie to make the voyage as well. It was a sad occasion the evening that Sofie left home. I cried bitter tears because the nicest of my siblings would leave us. Mother followed Sofie to the city and even to the spot where the ship lay anchor. She wept when the boat left the harbor with her two dear daughters.

The departure was timed to avoid the forbidding rigors of the Atlantic that challenged voyagers earlier or later in any given year. Countless lives had been lost over the years as explorers and emigrants sought to reach the New World. "If crosses and tombstones could be erected on the water to indicate the resting places of (those) killed by savages or the elements, the routes of the emigrant vessels from Europe to America would long since have assumed the appearance of crowded cemeteries," German author and emigration authority Friedrich Kapp wrote.

A spring departure would also give the immigrants time to plant crops in the hopes that the harvests would help them to weather their first winter in the new land.

Before the *Incognito* lifted anchor, all of the passengers gathered on deck as Captain Christophersen, in fatherlike fashion, explained their duties and the crew's expectations of them. He stressed the importance of hygiene and cooperation. One of the passengers, Pastor Jacob Aall Ottesen, was called upon to ask God's blessing upon the voyage.

The *Incognito* initially encountered rough seas, followed in a matter of days by an extended calm. Each of these extremes made many of the passengers uneasy. They often went up on deck, braving cold temperatures, to check on the weather and other conditions. It soon became evident that the absence of strong winds to propel the vessel southwestward would extend the trip's duration.

"After setting a course for the English Channel, we were very unlucky with the wind and lay 14 weeks at sea, eight of them in the Atlantic," Jens Jacobsen Skoien wrote. "Sofie, little Ellen and I were well the whole way, but Gina stayed almost always in bed up to a few days before we reached New York."

Time passed slowly for most of the emigrants. Some of the men tried their hand at fishing. Many women brought along spinning wheels and looms. A handful of musicians brought accordions, fiddles and other instruments, performing from time to time for singers, dancers and cloggers. Children occupied themselves with games or listened to the storytellers.

Lifelong friendships were formed aboard the *Incognito*. There were at least two marriages during the voyage and two healthy babies brought into the world, as well as four newborns who died. Most people remained in good health, avoiding the scourges of cholera, typhus, typhoid fever, dysentery and measles that had plagued other vessels. However, some became seasick, marked by violent diarrhea, discharge of blood, exhaustion and swelling.

There are few accounts of the trip, but two of the passengers, brothers Kjel Bredesen Straete and Peder Bredesen Straete, described their experiences in an account shared by a descendant, Alice Bredeson Zweifel. They indicated that there were several deaths on the voyage. Bodies of the deceased were buried at sea, a practice that, in the case of the *Incognito*, attracted a following of sharks anxious to feed on the corpses.

Peder Bredesen Straete related the sad personal tale of his one-year-old daughter Karen's death three weeks into the journey. After the funeral, the infant's body was lowered with ropes and a board to the water's level. The grieving Straete and his wife, Olia Knudsdatter Straete, looked on as one rope was then lifted to enable the body to slide gently into the water, where they were aghast to witness sharks instantly consume the little girl's remains.

They were consoled by Jacob Ottesen. The 27-year-old pastor and his wife of just one month, Catharina, were bound for the Norwegian community of Manitowoc in Wisconsin on a mission for Norwegian-Lutheran Church. A native of Nedre Romerike, Ottesen had earned a theology degree and was a schoolteacher in Christiania when he decided to set sail for America. He was described in one Lutheran publication as "a man of simple piety, humanistic tastes, and keen humor, a tenacious controversialist and grimly purposeful leader."

Passenger lists have been published, but are fraught with misspellings, gaps and contradictions that have long frustrated historians and genealogists. In most cases, the signature of a husband to a registry was all that was expected and spellings were sometimes altered during transcriptions or translations. These problems have challenged researchers attempting to compile lists of ship passengers, let alone entire colonial developments such as Oleana.

Some of the passengers on the 1852 voyage signed a recommendation for the *Incognito* and Captain Christophersen. They were: Berger Eriksen Sagerud, H. Wulfsberg, N. Tyrholm, Ole Olsen Knudsmoen, O. Syversen, M. Hersleth, A. B. Ulsbøl, C. Sjølie, A. Johannesen, I. Moe, Tosten T. Forkerud, H. F. Koss, Ole Olsen Hollet, Eberhardt Pedersen,

L. C. Prydz, A. Amundsen, Ped. E. Lømo, Forhenv Skolelærer, Kjel Bredesen Straete, Strette Blonken, Iver Olsen, O. Steffensen Stræte, Halvor Halvorsen, H. Soemerud, Matis Charlsen Juberget, Ole Syversen Snapholt, Martinius Olsen Snapholt, Brede Enersen Knudtsmoen, Tolef Tostensen Sjøli, Mical Olsen Snapholt, Ole Larsen Sorkness, Peder Bredesen Straete, Isak Hansen, P. Larsen, Ole Hansen, Carl Olsen, Anders Olsen Juberget, Paul Jansen, Peder Andersen Spenbyqvaern and Christian Olsen Sigerud.

The *Incognito* arrived in New York on Sept. 11. In accordance with the immigration laws, passengers were forbidden to leave the ship until they had made travel arrangements and had visited a quarantine station for medical examination. As soon as they disembarked, the ship owner had no further responsibility for them.

After the ship dropped anchor, Pastor Ottesen administered Holy Communion to most of the passengers and recorded their names as follows. Wulfber 1, Tyrholm 1, Koss 1, Johannesen 2, Syversen 1, Prytz 1, Amundsen 1, Krogsrud 1, Andreas Bergerson 2, Bernt Bergersen 1, Kjel Bredesen 1, Peder Bredesen 2, Jens Skøyen 2, Mathias Carlsen 2, Carl Mathisen 1, Mathis Mathisen 1, Marthin Bredesen 1, Cari Mathisdatter 1, Ole Pedersen 1, Peder Andersen 1, Hellene Pedersdatter 1, Arne Kjelsen 2, Ebrat Pedersen 1, Anders Olsen 2, Anna Thomasdatter 1, Ole Bredesen 1, Ole Larsen 1, Oleane Larsdatter 1, Carl Carlsen 2, Maren Olsdatter 1, Michel Olsen 2, Matheas Michelsen 1, Oluf Olsen 2, Ole Syversen 1, Goro Syversdatter 1, Daniel Eriksen 2, Syver Iversen 1, Marthin Olsen 2, Torsten Tørisen 2, Andreas Bronken 1, Peder Lømo 1, Halvor Halvorsen 1, Christian Olsen 1, Brede Enersen 1, Iver Olsen 1, Knut Olsen 1, Even Olsen 2, Ole Hansen 2, Isak Hansen 1, Peder Larsen 2, Carl Olsen 2, Anne Marie Larsdatter 1, Johanne Larsdatter 1, Peder Avlesen 1.

Within hours of their arrival, the *Incognito* passengers were also visited by a man of celebrity status: Ole Bull. He and John Nathaniel Holfeldt boarded the vessel to promote the New Norway colony and offer incentives for those immigrants willing to join them. Holfeldt was a 35-year-old Norwegian who had sailed to America in 1846 and become an emigrant agent, based in Wisconsin. He was also working as an accountant and printing supervisor for the Scandinavian Press Agency in the modern-day Orfordville (then Inmansville),Wisc., when he agreed to assist Bull in his efforts to populate the Oleana colony. Jens Jacobsen Skoien described the duo's arrival on the anchored *Incognito*:

After this long trip you can understand that we were very happy to get to the America land in one piece. So soon as we came to land we got ourselves together and we walked up in the city to look around. Luckily, my wife got her energy back and was able to be with us. You can believe that New York is a big city with much to see and I had good thoughts about the city.

As soon as we came into New York's harbor comes one called Holfeldt and Ole Bull onboard to offer us good land in Pennsylvania that Bull has bought to colonize Norwegians, Swedes and Danes. The offer was that everyone would be able to own 50 acres of land at $3 an acre, but pay (for it) with two work days every month for three years. To begin with, you would earn $15 a month and this would include meals and free house. Later, this would change to $1 a day and free house with your own food.

Skoien was among the many passengers persuaded to abandon their plans to settle in the Midwest or South. Lured by the promise of inexpensive land, a comfortable lifestyle and the possibilities of riches due to the presence of gold and other mineral wealth in the hills of Pennsylvania, a majority of the immigrants agreed to board the passenger railroad cars for the trip to Wellsville, N.Y., from which wagons would carry them on to New Norway.

Pastor Ottesen was among those who were intrigued by Bull's plan. Feeling a kinship with the passengers, he agreed to join Bull, Holfeldt and Captain Christophersen for a visit to the property, and to conduct religious services at Oleana while Bull sought a full-time clergyman.

Although Norway had abolished laws restricting religious freedom, persecution and discrimination were still factors in Norwegian emigration. The church embodied certain democratic elements and was a unifying force. Therefore, a clergyman was an influential figure, his position commanding respect even from men and women whose attitude toward religion was indifferent or hostile.

Prior to leaving New York, Bull was the guest of honor at a Scandinavian group's party at Claremont Hotel. He was applauded for his colony, which the toastmaster described as a "good deed." Ole assured the group that any Scandinavian who came to him—Norwegian, Danish or Swedish—would find "a warm heart and helpful hand." He then called for a toast to "man's most important good— freedom."

Word of Bull's plan spread. The *Philadelphia Bulletin* reported:

We observe, among the arrivals today, the name Ole Bull, the renowned Norwegian violinist, and learn on inquiry that he has just returned from a tour to the western part of this state, where he has purchased a large body of land on which he designs to establish a colony of his countrymen, the hardy, industrious people of Norway.

Ole Bull has shown his proverbial good sense in selecting a site for his colony in the rich unoccupied lands of Pennsylvania. The mineral and agricultural resources yet to be developed in that region will handsomely reward them for their labor and the state, in turn, will be benefited by the acquisition of so many inhabitants of a class so well known to be industrious and useful members of a community as the Norwegians.

An even more glowing and flowery account appeared in the influential *New York Times* edition of Sept. 25, 1852, excerpted here:

Not unimportant is the Norwegian colony, which the distinguished Northman, Ole Bull, has for some time been intending to establish, and has now begun. In a former visit, some seven years since, he traversed the United States. At that time, he formed an ardent attachment to the Republic, her institutions, and her people. He desired to see some of his hardy countrymen withdrawn from this cold and reluctant soil, from which they compelled a scanty subsistence, and planted in a home on the broad and fertile acres of America, with all the privileges of citizenship and all the rights of freemen.

The tendency of Norwegian emigration, hitherto, has been directed mainly to Wisconsin, where already about forty thousand of these sons of the North have taken the oath of allegiance. But the ravages of disease, the long distance from market, and the grasping of the surrounding lands by speculators have made this section in some important respects undesirable.

Ole Bull has been industriously laboring to find a more advantageous position and has, we think, succeeded in the large tract of land he has secured for this purpose in the southern part of Potter County, Pennsylvania. The territory selected is well adapted to the purpose. It is not a worn-out and cast-off tract, nor have its energies been at all exhausted in the support of a previous population. But it is a virgin and vigorous soil, innocent of hoe or plow, with the accumulated fertility of former years, sustaining original forests, and tenanted by those anti-aborigines, the prowling wolf, the antlered deer, and surly bear.

It is a fine, rolling country, swelling up from a rich valley, with hills that have almost outgrown the name, and having in one body some twelve thousand acres of table land. It is salubrious, heavily timbered, well watered, and holds salt springs and deposits of coal and iron. In the formation, products and animals of this region, the colonists will be continually reminded of their native Norway. The delicious mountain trout with which its streams abound will recall to them many a pleasant reminiscence.

The region has hitherto remained sequestered and inaccessible. It was beyond the ken of civilization. The descendants of its first occupants still roamed the wilderness, or plied their fins within its cool waters. But now the track of that great railroad—the New York and Erie—which unites the waves of Lake Erie with the Atlantic billows—winds within 30 miles of its northern bounds; and on the southern within 15 miles, the unearthly scream of the steam whistle, on the Pennsylvania road, affrights the air. It has thus been suddenly brought out from its concealment and remoteness, made accessible, and placed within a convenient distance of markets.

What an element in the wealth, strength and resources of our country will be these Scandinavian brains and muscle when two or three thousand people shall fill those now tenantless fields! Such a population—stout and vigorous, accustomed to economy, endurance and toil, and glowing with aspirations for freedom—is indeed to be coveted, to raise the note of civilization amidst the silence of the woods. We doubt not, they will bring with them the glorious motto which, in pride of their barren summits, they stamp upon their rix dollars, "Truth, Honor and Loyalty are found among the mountains of Norway."

We are glad to see this child of genius identify himself and his interests with the Western world. To a lady who, in reference to his tall and muscular figure remarked that he was a Norwegian pine, Bull replied, "Yes, but I am about to become an American pine: will you give me room to grow and cultivate me?" We think this will be cheerfully accorded to him. Certainly no artist has ever visited us whom we would more earnestly greet. Full of generous and ardent impulses, of pleasant companionship, wielding the highest powers of music, and with his heart in his hand, we rejoice that he has undertaken the great task of transplanting a colony of Northmen (himself included) into American soil.

Let him bring his Cremona from its case again and tender to the people over the country a succession of concerts in aid of his enterprise, and to afford facilities to the humbler classes of his countrymen to leave their sterile acres for this new Norway, and we should suppose that the benevolence of his undertaking, the genius of his bow, and the real benefit to our country would crown his efforts with distinguished success.

Seven

Ole Bull's dream of developing a New Norway in the Pennsylvania mountains generated great excitement among the residents of Potter County. However, many found it odd that Bull would choose an area with such steep terrain for the development of a colony to be supported primarily by agriculture. Still, most were inclined to give him the benefit of the doubt and wished him well.

Pastor Ottesen described the trip from New York to Oleana in this letter to a friend in Norway:

(The captain and I) left the ship in New York at 5:00 a.m. September 17 in the morning, and met Ole Bull and Holfeldt by the steamboat. The steamboat took us over the Hudson River to New Jersey and we took the train. The train is like a big salon, with 20 sofas on both sides of a narrow corridor. With two people in every sofa, the train could take 80 persons, and none of them knew the famous artist Ole Bull. Here, you would not find art, poetry or science, only dollars and steam— that is it.

In New Jersey and New York, the first states we went through, we saw the richest and greenest vegetation I could imagine. New York has splendid fruit and herb gardens, and when we now know that they serve fruit with the poorest meal, we understand that they need large deliveries. We were served melons, cantaloupes and peaches at all restaurants, even apple pie and other baked goods. I asked them how they use all of the Indian corn and pumpkins we passed by, and the answer was to feed the people. On one of the stations we passed, tables were prepared for 500 people. For 25 cents you got beef, turkey, ham, and coffee and tea. But the coffee was thin as tea, and the tea thin as water. And the cream was barely milk.

Next morning, from 7:00 in the morning to 7:30 in the evening, we drove 367 miles through lovely fields with hills and small rivers and villages with white houses and gardens in front. By Genesee, we left the train and drove to a small place, Wellsville, where we stayed overnight. They had 20 rooms and we got our own. Yes, we lived as gentlemen, and no stranger has ever given me this much. But it was Bull who wanted me to preach for his colony, and that was the reason why I came in the first place.

From Wellsville, we left at 5 in the morning, driving in a covered wagon. In the woods as we passed, houses and farmland became more seldom, while the pine trees grew bigger and bigger . . . It was really nice to meet the immigrants again. Both men and women cried when they saw the captain and me again, and I was happy to promise solemnity over their new homes. I think they appreciated me. My blessing started like this: 'No one can serve two masters. Look first for the Lord.' All of them were moved and I hope the Lord can bless their hearts.

The arrival of the first wave of colonists, some 105 men, women and children, caused a considerable stir in Coudersport. A trial in the Potter County Courthouse was recessed so that participants could witness the spectacle as dozens of colorfully clad newcomers arrived by wagons and circulated among the locals. The "warm heart and helpful hand" that Bull had promised was quickly extended by Coudersport's populace. The town's two hotels did not have enough rooms to accommodate all of the guests, so despite the awkward language and cultural differences, many of the families were welcomed into local residents' homes.

Nine-year-old Burt Olson told about his first meal in Coudersport.

He had never tasted "green corn," which was placed at every table, but became fond of it and ate so much that he became ill.

The following morning, much to the delight of the visitors and townspeople alike, Ole Bull himself appeared on the front steps of the Coudersport Hotel, site of the present Hotel Crittenden in downtown Coudersport. He charmed the onlookers with an impromptu violin performance.

The Norwegians visited local businesses to purchase lumber, stoves, household items and other provisions. Their belongings loaded by late morning, they started down the Coudersport and Jersey Shore Turnpike toward the Kettle Creek valley. Some paid extra to have a larger volume of belongings transported by separate wagon. Older members of the group, most of the women and the very young rode in wagons, while the more able-bodied set out on foot for the 30-mile trek to join the Oleana workmen.

Economic arrangements in the colony's early days called for Ole Bull to pay each worker who cleared land or built cabins 50 cents in American currency each day. Skilled laborers were to be paid slightly more. Bull also agreed to supply food and other provisions for the early settlers and to allow them rent-free occupancy in the cabins until they could build their own homes and begin to support themselves by growing crops.

A price of $2.50 to $3.00 per acre was established for colonists who wished to purchase their own lots of 25 to 50 acres; Bull was willing to accept installment payments of $2.00 per month until the sale price was met, at which time the deed would be conveyed.

Songs and ballads spread throughout Norway, reflecting the hopes and dreams of those whose chose to leave. One popular ballad beckoned emigrants to Oleana:

Good men of Norway, strong of arm,
If fortune's barbs have torn you,
Behold a friend whose heart is warm,

A man who will not scorn you.
Better he than gold or fame!
Ole Bull— yes, that's his name.

He knows that here are grief and pain,
Your burdens he would lighten.
Freedom, bread— these you will gain,
Your future he will brighten.
Better he than gold or fame!
You know him— Ole Bull's his name!

Robert Hamilton, a surveyor from Chatham Run in Clinton County, south of the Norwegian colony, was hired by Bull and Cowan to develop detailed plans for four "cities." The site of today's Carter Camp at the northernmost section of Bull's holdings was designated as New Bergen, named for the Norwegian city of Bull's birth. Oleana, by virtue of its central location, was envisioned as the colony's cultural and commercial hub. Not far to the south was New Norway, in the vicinity of today's Ole Bull State Park. Overlooking that village was a mountainside "shelf" or "bench," chosen by Bull as the site of his own home. In the southernmost stretches of the Norwegian settlement was a section of the Kettle Creek valley designated as the village of "Valhalla." In Norse mythology, Valhalla was the place of Odin, the god of poetry, who received military heroes when they were slain in battle.

Bull fully expected that New Bergen, Oleana, New Norway and Valhalla would evolve into communities where residents would gather for social functions, church services and school classes, while working the farmland in the outlying areas surrounding each village. The plan was greeted warmly by the Norwegians as long as Bull's enthusiasm—and his money—held out.

Any number of community facilities would be built to complement the vast stretches of forests that were to be cleared to accommodate agriculture. Bull saw no limit to how far the Norwegian settlement could be expanded through additional land purchases. He told one excited audience in Williamsport, Pennsylvania, in September 1852 that he intended "to bring tens of thousands of my oppressed countrymen to this free and happy land."

Pastor Ottesen had some immediate concerns upon his arrival, as shared in this letter he sent to an acquaintance back in Norway:

> *He wants to colonize a settlement with Norwegian immigrants called New Norway. Construction has already begun in a section he calls Oleana. Here he has a flag consisting of the Norwegian and American colors, and by the help of some American speculators' capital he is beginning in grand style. About two-thirds of all the Norwegians (on the* Incognito*) made for this place.*
>
> *Ole Bull expects ultimately to get the whole of this impenetrable forest with its steep hillsides turned into cultivated land, inhabited by our countrymen. I must say that I advise no one take my word for granted, as I do not yet know whether he CAN keep his promise and realize his great plans. Poor people get a better situation under his protection, but whether it is advisable to buy land here, I do now know.*
>
> *It appears to me that the forest is so dense and the hillsides so steep that it can scarcely become good arable land, but good only for cattle grazing, and especially good for goats. Wild cherry trees are everywhere and a black pine, called hemlock, is so big you cannot even embrace it. I am firmly of the belief that Ole Bull means well, but he is no businessman, and added thereto are politico-democratic plans wholesale in the scheme also. Oleana lies sixty miles from the railway...*

Bull had, in fact, been led to believe that two rail lines would be extended to connect his colony to commercial centers, one from the north and one from the south. Pastor Otteson remained in Pennsylvania for only a few weeks before departing for his Wisconsin destination. Given a pastor's role in the lives of immigrant communities, Ottesen's departure was a serious blow, but he was destined for greater things.

Ottesen's writings reflected the views of many colonists who questioned the feasibility of developing farmland out of such heavily forested acres, on steep terrain. However, no one would not have sensed any skepticism or concern from reading the Sept. 24, 1852, edition of the *People's Journal* in Coudersport:

We have heard from (the colonists) two and three times since, and they all seem delighted with their location. We are much pleased at their cheerfulness; for these hardy sons of Norway are just what is needed to subdue our vast forests; and we are very confident that the benefit will be mutual; for our land in its wild state is very cheap, but when cleared and improved is as productive as any in the state. Hence, it is so very easy for a laboring man, though ever so poor, to become, in his new country, independent.

To some of the emigrants, the desire for political and cultural independence, as well as the prospects of wealth, were strong enough to compel them to risk everything. "Ever so poor" described the majority of the New Norway settlers, but some were relatively well off. Among the colonists were college graduates, building contractors and other Norwegians who had sold their homes or farms to finance their expensive trip. Observers in Coudersport took note of fine furniture, musical instruments, spinning wheels and looms loaded on the wagons bound for Oleana.

Several weeks after he wrote it, Pastor Ottesen's letter was published in a Norwegian newspaper, accompanied by these opinions by a similarly prophetic editor:

It is easy to understand that this area is surrounded by high hills covered with forests, as the letter-writer says. This can explain why this district, surrounded by the oldest and most populated regions in America, has been empty until this day. We are not told about Bull's relationship to the American speculators, who invested their money in this project.

Who were the owners of the land? Was Ole Bull only their agent? Since American businessmen use all ideas and feelings in the interest of speculation, and turn it into valuable money, both may be true.

Also, it is not a good sign that none of the passengers knew Ole Bull on the train. Was he already forgotten in America as the big artist? If he had gotten the rights to 120,000 acres not far from New York, capitalists would have known . . . We must express our worries about how Ole Bull's fortune and reputation will survive this transaction, since he is dealing with smarter people than himself.

We do not think it likely that this case will raise problems for our countrymen. Fifteen dollars a day is a good salary for immigrants. If the payment is not paid timely, we assume the worker will leave the place. Hopefully, they will get to know the place and the soil well enough to not pay 10, five or three dollars per acre if it is not worth it.

Whether the company will make money does not depend entirely on the sale of the land, but also the value of the land. The letter-writer admired the hemlock spruce, and an English expert says that this type is very typical in northern America. In the United States, however, it is only observed in the Allegheny Mountains, by creeks and naked cliffs. It is very beautiful as young, but when it gets older, the enormous branches snap under heavy snow. Its logs have small value, since it is neither lasting nor fresh and is used mainly as coarse wood.

But New Norway and Oleana is existing, something Norwegians must not forget. The colony has established contact with the Democratic Party, which can support General Pierce's chances in the Presidential election, but more important their connections to Ole Bull's world-known reputation. This is also the place to meet fellow countrymen, which might lead the immigration stream from Wisconsin to Pennsylvania.

That some of the colonists' expectations may not have been realistic is suggested by this description from writer George M. Stephenson in his article, entitled "The Mind of the Scandinavian Immigrant":

The industry of the Scandinavian is proverbial; but in some instances his mind reacted unfavorably to the hard work expected of him in America. It required some adjustment to get in step with the speedy army of American working men. "Many are under the impression that if they can only get to America everything needed will come as a matter of course— but the opposite is truth," wrote a journeyman blacksmith from Norway. "The work is harder than anything experienced in Norway: early and late one must work to earn one's bread."

Others admitted that they never knew what hard work was until they stooped their necks to the yoke in America, but there was a certain pride in the admission. There was something about the great distances in America, the hustle and bustle, the "go-ahead" spirit, the rapidly growing communities and cities, plus the ownership of a farm and a bank account in the future, that buoyed them up and eventually made them victims of that American optimism which makes every town "the best town in the best county in the best state in the best country in the world."

The concept of "ownership" would prove to be a key distinction in the case of the Oleana colony. At the outset, Ole Bull didn't actually own any of the land on which the settlers began building in September 1852. No deeds had been filed to make the change in ownership official. As an alien who was considered a subject of the Kingdom of Norway and Sweden, Bull could not legally hold or convey property of more than 5,000 acres in Pennsylvania. His associates made plans to rectify the situation by having Bull take out "first papers" to become an official citizen of the United States. In the meantime, the "colonial development company" was responsible for the operation of the colony while the necessary paperwork was processed.

Applying for citizenship was traditionally a routine matter, but not for Ole Bull. He insisted upon a formal ceremony at historic Independence Hall in Philadelphia, directly under the statue of George Washington. This may have been meant to send a message to the national leaders of Norway, or to gain publicity for the colony.

With John Cowan by his side, Bull left Oleana by one-horse buggy, bound for Williamsport, where he would spend the night before continuing on to Philadelphia. Encouraged by city leaders, Bull agreed to present a solo concert in the Lycoming County Courthouse. As word of the performance spread, every seat of the courtroom was filled and the crowd overflowed into the stairways and outside the entrance.

His large white hat protruding among the dignitaries assembled on a makeshift stage, Bull was introduced by native son Cowan, who proclaimed, "Ladies and gentlemen— permit me to introduce you to the world renowned Ole Bull. He appears before you not only as the great artist, but as an adopted citizen of the West Branch valley. Within a few weeks, he has purchased from me 120,000 acres of land in Potter County. He intends to bring thousands of his hardy and industrious countrymen to occupy and cultivate that land. If his life is spared, within the next five years, he will be the efficient means of adding thousands to the population of Northern Pennsylvania, and hundreds of thousands to its wealth. Need I say more?"

Bull's performance was reviewed by a reporter with the local newspaper, the *Williamsport Democrat*:

You might as well attempt to imprison the gorgeous colors of the rainbow as attempt to give a description of Ole Bull's playing. You are lost, bewildered, astonished, captivated! Surely that instrument he holds must have a heart and soul, and all the other attributes of our spiritual nature, for those sounds cannot be produced by the friction of catgut and horsehair! He gives, as it were, an embodiment to every emotion of the heart— touching the deep wells of affection and reaching the consuming fire of the passions.

At times you are listening to the warbling of the birds, the soft sight of the summer wind as it woos the quivering leaf, or the pleasant flow of waters. The next moment, you are transported to the cold, bleak, fearful wilds of Norway to hear the roar of foaming cataracts and to listen to the solemn surge of the sea as it beats against a rockbound coast. Again, you are in another and more genial clime, in the midst of a carnival, watching the tricks and smiling at the mirth of the beautiful but degraded children of the sunny South.

At length, Ole Bull ceased playing; but the audience moved not, for "Listening still, they seem to hear." Bull, finally, made a movement for the door, when the audience rose and gave him three hearty, honest cheers, loud enough and strong enough to have raised the roof off the Court House.

Bull and Cowan boarded their buggy the next morning and continued their trip toward Philadelphia, where the citizenship ceremony took place on Sept. 25. With his counselors John M. Reed and John O'Brien accompanying him, Bull placed his right hand over his heart and declared, "I desire to be deemed worthy of so great a privilege. I will do everything in my power to fulfill my promise. I have never sworn allegiance to the King of Norway and Sweden nor to any other potentate, nor have I bowed the knee to any but my God."

Pointing upward with his left hand, his face beaming, Bull continued: "I shall value the privilege of citizenship above every other earthly object. I shall endeavor to introduce hundreds of thousands of my countrymen to so great a boon that they may also feel the great difference between being a citizen of this glorious republic, in the full enjoyment of liberty, and that of the state of existence in which they now find themselves. Already have a thousand Norwegians settled within the limits of this Commonwealth, in the northern part, and I hope that before another year expires, many thousands more will taste the blessings of liberty in the same locality. I shall not cease my efforts until all the Norwegians who wish to emigrate shall be in the full possession of their natural rights, and in the enjoyment of a farm in Pennsylvania."

Reminding the crowd of the Norse discovery of America, Bull then recited the oath required by law and signed his citizenship papers. He acceded to the welcoming committee's request for a violin performance. A journalist at the scene wrote of Bull's playing as "an embodiment of every emotion of the heart— touching the deep wells of affection and reaching the consuming fire of the passions . . . He is a man with lots of compassion, burning for human rights. He will become a great citizen of the republic."

Ironically, despite the grandeur of the occasion and the uproar that the ceremony would cause in Norway, Ole Bull's citizenship never became official. He failed to remain in America for the six years necessary to obtain a final decree and, thus, did not file the required second set of certification papers. He was, however, granted specific rights to own real property by the Pennsylvania General Assembly.

Bull returned to Oleana following the ceremony in Philadelphia. His colony continued to attract the attention of Norwegian and U.S. newspapers. John Nathaniel Holfeldt, the emigrant agent, parlayed his Scandinavian Press Agency connections into an article in *Emigranten* giving a rosy description of the colony.

The book *America, Ole Bull and New Norway,* most likely commissioned by Bull and published anonymously in Norway, tried to build enthusiasm for the colony. It told of America's legal and school systems, as well as general economic and social conditions in the country. It also contained a section on Bull's first American visit, a chapter on slavery entitled "Uncle Tom's Cabin," and extensive promotional information about Oleana. Here's an excerpt:

Here in the old world, freedom is but a name; hence this busy stir toward the distant port. For the land there in the West is free both for belief and for practice and the answers to many difficult problems may be found there. America! For a long time Norway's sons have been making their way to your blossoming fields to build for themselves new homes; but often, upon landing on your beautiful shores, joyfully and with hope, they have been deceived by fair words. Hurrah for the master of the strings, Ole Bull! He has now taken this stand among you, firm against hatred and strife. He is founding a New Norway for the benefit of his countrymen, which amply blessed with peace and freedom will make men marvel.

A review of the book in the Feb. 17, 1853, *Christiania-Posten* reflected the capital city's growing skepticism about Oleana. The writer described it as "a work from which it is hoped the publisher will have as little profit as he has honor." Newspapers in Bergen were much more friendly toward Bull, as was *Arbeider-Foreningernes Blad*, the organ of the labor movement. The latter declared that hundreds of thousands would be willing to leave Norway on Ole Bull's word alone, due to the government's anti-labor attitude. They would "sing farewell my valley and farewell my mountain, long have I been a miserable slave. But now, with a free mind and a full heart, I am setting off for Ole Bull."

Bull's reputation was further boosted in his homeland by a second major Bull biography, authored by Henrik Winter-Hjelm.

One of his harshest critics was Ditmar Meidell, editor of a humor magazine, *Krydseren*. Mocking Ole's compulsion over the Viking discovery of America, Meidell suggested that Norwegians take over all of America and divide the country into such states as Oleana, Mariana, Larsiana and Pauliana. On Nov. 20, 1852, he wrote, "So far as Ole Bull is concerned, it may be conceded that he can play the violin, but this hardly implies that with his bow he can level the earth, move mountains and clear primeval forests."

As scattered snow flurries heralded the coming winter, small groups of cabins, most of them housing multiple families, had been erected in the villages of Oleana and New Bergen. Mortimer Smith described this phase of the colony's development:

(Bull) arose early in the morning, and seated on his magnificent horse he was everywhere, directing the work and encouraging the colonists with vivid word pictures of the utopia he was planning for them. They listened with quiet wonder to his visionary discourses and were duly impressed; but sometimes these simple peasants from home were a little puzzled by some of the great man's ideas.

It is doubtful if Bull had formulated any consistent idea of what he wanted to do at Oleana, but it is certain that he thought of himself as the head of the little empire he was building, for all his life he had longed to be the man of action, the benevolent dictator who out of his superior wisdom would guide weaker and simpler men to a satisfactory way of life.

Locals looked on with polite curiosity as a couple of the colonists were seen wearing high silk hats, ivory white when new. In one of his flights of fancy, Bull had purchased upwards of 150 of these hats from a New York millinery and stocked them at a little store at Oleana. Ole had hoped the colonists might adopt the white high hat as some sort of official headgear, but it was not well suited to men whose job was chopping down trees and building houses.

Not all of the settlers were focused on clearing property and building cabins. Sightings of Native Americans from the Allegheny Reservation along the turnpike or in the forests fueled speculation of gold or silver in the mountains of southern Potter County. Excavations by the colonists were unsuccessful, but their remnants can still be found in the hillsides surrounding the colonial settlements.

With colder weather arriving, Bull was anxious to have the 20-acre experimental garden and nursery established on the Kettle Creek "island" south of the New Norway area. Some 1,100 fruit trees were brought to the plot by surveyor Robert Hamilton. John Cowan, on Bull's behalf, approved payment of $100 out of the violinist's account for the trees and promised Hamilton that the remaining $89 due would be forthcoming soon. This relatively minor transaction is important in two respects— it demonstrates Cowan's close involvement with the day-to-day financial management of the colony, and it suggests that Bull was running out of money, even in late 1852. Expenses for settlement of the land had far exceeded projections, as evidenced by several letters that Cowan wrote to the colonists and others, emphasizing the need to control costs.

In one letter, Cowan advised Hamilton to "pay no attention to the

Norwegians about their notions of fixing things, as most of them of the lower place (Oleana) will probably leave and a great number of new ones come in the Spring . . . If any of the Norwegians are dissatisfied, advise them to go to work on the Williamsport & Elmira Railroad. Let them select their land before they go. Mr. Bull will be ready to execute deeds as soon as you can get the surveys ready."

Aware of his worsening financial plight, Ole Bull turned to what he knew best—his violin—to rebuild his fortune and support the colony. He was highly regarded in the U.S. and would have no trouble selling out concert appearances wherever he chose to perform. That November, Bull teamed with Maurice Strakosch, a 27-year-old tall and drooping pianist who served as his accompanist and concert manager. They were joined by Strakosch's stepdaughter, ten-year-old singer Adelina Patti, billed as an eight-year-old in order to make her vocal talents seem even more remarkable.

Although Bull enjoyed playing with the child during his off-hours, he also considered her to be spoiled and undisciplined. This is confirmed by Maurice Strakosch. Among his anecdotes was an account of the child's tantrum when Bull refused to allow her to refill her champagne glass at the dinner table, culminating with the girl slapping Ole in the cheek. On another occasion, in Albany, N.Y., Adelina refused to sing unless she were given a bag of candy, forcing Strakosch to track down a confectioner while Bull was buying time onstage with an extended version of "Carnival of Venice."

Trouble was brewing back at Oleana. In a letter posted Nov. 11, 1852, from Carter Camp, one of the colony's managers, Elling Larsen, detailed some of the problems he had observed since Bull's departure:

Honorable countryman and benefactor:

Please excuse me for bothering you with this letter, but I find it necessary for my own sake to inform you, that from the first time I came here I found some domineering elements among the managers. They seemed to be against Paulsen, but I think that he was more on your side than any of the rest. I noticed that I was not welcome here either at first. I was spied on and examined up and down. They asked me why I came here and what I was to do; however, they soon found out what I was to do, when goods arrived for me. They again tried to make trouble for me, but I told them that I had received goods before and that I knew very well how to handle them. Unfortunately, the goods were not accompanied by an invoice, and I had to start selling them without knowing what they would cost me, which was probably lucky for me.

Today I have again received more goods, for which I received an invoice and I also received the invoice for the first shipment, but I had to defend my rights, as they were trying to go too far. I have always tried to satisfy the people and I shall continue to do so as long as I can, so that you shall not be blamed, when you have tried to do so much for me and all your countrymen. I shall only ask that you do not allow the Germans to have the same power in New Bergen that they had in old Bergen.

Abbott has moved out and I have moved into the house he occupied, and I intend to purchase the house and the land surrounding same. Friends have told me that Daun had said that I could move in, but that by summertime he would get me out again, and that he was going to write to you about something. I would therefore ask you that you do nothing in this matter until you have considered it well, and I am sure that you will do this.

Expressing my sincere gratitude, I remain
Respectfully yours,
Elling Larsen

There is no indication that Bull responded to the Larsen letter. He continued on the concert tour, where his performances were well attended and profitable. Appearances in St. Louis and several cities in upstate New York—along with relaxation at Saratoga Springs, N.Y., with, among others, author Washington Irving—preceded a Christmas celebration with the Longfellows in Cambridge.

He met William Makepeace Thackery during this visit, as confirmed by the writer himself: "I had a very pleasant little party-kin last night at Cambridge at Longfellows', where there was a madcap fiddler Ole Bull, who played most wonderfully on his instrument, and charmed me still more by his oddities and character. Quite a character for a book."

The colonists observed the holiday without their leader present. "The Christmas holiday was celebrated as best they could, with as much encouragement and cheerful hearts as the situation allowed for," wrote Torstein Jahr, a librarian with the Library of Congress who studied the Bull colony in detail a half-century after its demise. "The first Christmas away from home and family is always sad, and they missed the comfort Ole Bull's presence would have given them."

Jens Jacobsen Skoien's letter of Jan. 16, 1853, expressed the hope and confidence still held by many of the colonists. "The land here is very fertile and produces impressive corn and vegetables, but the fields lay between carved out valleys that are strongly overgrown with forest. There you will find in the woods oak, raspberry, walnut, maple and evergreen, and the trees are much bigger than you would find in the woods at home. Here is land enough to select, that Ole Bull owns 300,000 acres . . . and I believe that I have been fortunate with the selection of land. So, soon as the snow goes away in the Spring, I will build us a home."

Skoien wrote optimistically of roads being built and plans for the construction of a church. "I am feeling at peace," he said. "I can say with assurance that I would ten times rather be here than in Norway. The climate is so good and we have all been healthy. But I must make clear that this is not a place for just anyone who feels like coming to change Norway for America. For the older people there is no support here; no one can help them at the beginning. This is a place for people in their best years who can and will work and have a desire to earn money. Those who want to come should sail with Capt. Christophersen and bring potatoes, canned herring, flatbread and other food, as well as clothing."

No Norwegian would have another chance to ride with Christophersen on his *Incognito*. After a brief stay at Oleana, the captain returned to New York. He and his crew set out to sea carrying cargo bound for Europe. On Feb. 2, 1853, the newspaper *Morgenbladet* in Christiania reported: "There has lately been a lot of concern here in town about the brig *Incognito*. It was October 2 last year executed from New York to set sail for Antwerp. No information has been reported by the 24th of January. Consequently, after 114 days, apparently it was 'lost with man and mouse'."

Another colonist, identified only as H. Larsen, wrote to *Morgenbladet*: "We all know the North's great artist, but we shall soon learn to know the North's great benefactor . . . He has bought so much land that it can receive our countrymen for many years, even should emigration become many times as large as it hitherto has been; and every industrious and good man can look forward with certainty to a carefree and happy home."

Bull and the other musicians headed to Cincinnati and then embarked on a month-long engagement in New Orleans. Although Bull heard little about his colony during the tour, the plight of the Norwegians in Pennsylvania was not far from his mind. He made repeated references to his performances as "farewell concerts," not because he was planning to return to Norway, but because he was considering giving up his career, perhaps to pursue a political agenda. A large portion of the concert proceeds were sent directly to John Cowan to support the settlers.

Eventually, bitterness over Bull's diversion of immigrants to Pennsylvania spilled over into the pages of the *Milwaukee Free Democrat*:

It is well known that each successive year witnesses a large emigration from Norway to this country. The Norwegians are industrious, frugal, intelligent and moral, and are a very desirable class of emigrants. Hitherto a large portion of them have found their way to Wisconsin, adding largely to the industry, wealth and good character of our Commonwealth. It is also very important to the interests of our state that this emigration should continue.

But a strong effort has been made the past season to divert the current of this emigration to Pennsylvania. Ole Bull, of horse hair and cat-

gut celebrity, has undertaken to settle a large colony of his countrymen in Potter County, Pa. There is doubtless good land in Potter County, but this has been appropriated, long ago. The unsettled portion is notorious for its poor soil, being hilly, timbered with hemlock, and of a soil so notoriously sterile that the American farmer would not settle upon it, save in the last extremity. And this is the place where Ole Bull proposes to found a colony.

Jealousy or a desire for quick prosperity may have motivated that editorial, but its contents were not far from the truth. The editors of Potter County's *People's Journal*, unabashed boosters themselves, felt compelled to fire back:

The Democrat *is one of the best and most accurate papers with which we have the pleasure of an exchange, but the above article does great injustice to this county. The good land of this county has not all been appreciated. In fact, some of the best land in the county—land as good as can be found in western New York—is at this day an unbroken wilderness and offers to the industrious laborer inducements to settle on it as great as the best lands in Wisconsin. A large share of the unsettled portion of this county is good land and, since the completion of the New York & Erie Railroad, is settling fast.*

The reputation of Wisconsin land is worldwide; the fertility of the soil no one questions; her inviting prairies are rapidly filling up with hardy settlers. We don't see that her editors need envy the good luck which has at last set in the direction of Potter County. We hope the Democrat *will have the magnanimity to correct these erroneous statements.*

Potter County is not "proverbial for the amount of its sterile soil," and if it was, the proverb would be false. In fact, there is scarce a county in the state as free from the sterile soil as this much-abused county of Potter. It is "free soil" the Democrat *has heard of, and for what we are proud to say "Little Potter" is pre-eminent, being the banner county in the Keystone State, which position she is bound to maintain.*

Eight

With U.S citizenship comes taxation, so it was no surprise that the taxman would pay a call to the Oleana settlement in late 1852. He must have faced a considerable challenge in overcoming language barriers, spelling differences and the resentment of his very existence. In Norway, people were identified by a first (Christian) name, a patronymic and a farm name. The patronymic was usually based on the father's name. For boys, it ended in "sen" or "son," for girls in "datter" or "dotter." A farm name, derived from the place of residence, was subject to change if one moved.

This first assessment effort resulted in the following summary of the Norwegians and their holdings in the Abbott Township portion of Oleana; spellings are shown as officially recorded:

Henry Anderson, clerk, estimated value $200.

Workers Agust Amundsen, Andreas Brunker, Benct Bergesen and Ole Berdsen, each $50.

Ole Bull, 25 acres, at $5.00 each acre, total $125; seven houses at $50, total $350, corrected to $280; two horses at $50, total $100, corrected to $80; two bulls at $20, total $40; three cows at $12, total $36, corrected to $24; total of $651.

Workers Petter Andersen, Brede Enersen, Johannes Evensen, Daniel Eriksen, Save and Ole Eversen, Paul Ehonsen, Ens

Jacokbsen, Hans Holm, Ever Huberget, each $50.

Otto Kaas, teacher, $75.

Elling Lawson, 39 acres at $1.50, $58; house, $40; value of groceries, $300, corrected to $0; total of $398, corrected to $98.

Workers E. Kulmsee; Petter Lomo; Mathies and Carl Mathiesen; N. Nielsen; Jacob, Mathies and Ole Oluf; H.C, Andres and Christen Olsen; Ole Pedersen; Lars Prytz; Gustavus Skoyen; Tolef Tostensen and Tosten Torresen, each $50.

Olaus Solberg, baker, $75.

Niels Suher, house and property, $150; one cow, $12; total of $162

There's no way to determine how thorough or accurate this assessment was, so it provides only a vague glimpse at the population of one of the New Norway villages. Women and children were not recorded, nor were any settlers residing in the Stewardson Township portion of the colony.

To welcome their new neighbors, the publishers of the *People's Journal* on Dec. 10 printed this poem sent to them by Miss R. E. Daniels of Ulysses in northern Potter County:

Welcome the Norwegian band, a band so richly blest;
You're welcome to our native land if it will give you rest;
You're welcome to our home so rude, you're welcome to its cheer;
We do not think it an intrude; you are all welcome here.

You'll find there's joy in freemen's land,
And blessings smiling here;
We are a free and happy band,
You need to have no fear;
A noble band we know you are,
You'll find us just and true;
You've left your home and come so far,

We will be kind to you.

Our mountain home to us is dear—
Its rude romantic scenes—
Come on! Come! You're welcome here,
Where truth and love convene,
To make the heart that's sad with fear,
More blessed in our sweet land,
And drown the homesick sad'ning tear
Of the Norwegian band.

If death and sickness shall o'ertake
You in your newfound home,
You'll find that we will not forsake
And leave alone to mourn
Those friends who are bereft,
But shed a sympathetic tear.
Assure again, you are welcome here
To joys we call our own

We will give our cheers with cheerful heart
For your brave leader's merit;
Our love to him we will impart
And praise his noble spirit.
We know his mind is deep, profound—
He's welcome to our land!
We know his judgment to be sound.
He guards a noble band.

On behalf of the colonists, C. Wang sent this response on Dec. 23:

We are all of us very much obliged to you for your song of welcome to us Norwegians, offered in the People's Journal. *We are also gratified to hear having neighbors who sympathize in our fate; and we assure you, nothing will be spared by us to be good neighbors, as well as worthy citizens of this free and powerful Republic.*

Problems that had emerged in the colony's early days were festering as winter tightened its grip on the Kettle Creek valley. Many of the settlers were running out of money. Payments that Ole Bull had promised them for their labors were slow in coming, fueling suspicions among the colonists that Bull's business representatives had intercepted the money sent to Pennsylvania by the musician. Cowan, Hamilton and others involved in Bull's financial affairs were called upon to juggle a variety of debts incurred in the establishment and development of the settlement. There's no documentation to support the allegation that Bull's associates mishandled the funds. However, based on his tendency to pronounce himself a victim of others' wrongdoing or exploitation, Bull probably did little to discourage such speculation.

Some families who had the means to acquire food, clothing and other necessities shared with their less fortunate neighbors, as provisions became scant. Coudersport was 30 miles away and could be reached only when the road was cleared of the snow, which sometimes drifted to heights of six feet or more. More often than not, the road was impassable.

Colonists had to endure the monotony of their own cooking, many of them seldom tasting fresh meat, fruit or vegetables. Because the workday for many started at sunrise, the Norwegians had hearty appetites.

Such difficulties did not deter Ole Bull and John Holfeldt from recruiting. Holfeldt placed an advertisement in the Dec. 24, 1853, edition of *Emigranten* in Inmansville, Wisc., encouraging settlers who had already established residency in the Midwest to relocate to Oleana.

A handful of settlers left the colony in early January, seeking employment elsewhere, but still hoping to return. However, most of the colonists were determined to survive their first Pennsylvania winter and confident of the settlement's future.

A letter sent back home by Jens Jacobsen Skoien told of the

birth of a son to him and his wife Gina. Her sister Sofie accepted a housekeeping job for a local family, at a salary of $4.00 per month plus room and board.

A *People's Journal* story appearing in early January told of the colony's continued development:

We are happy for the message we got from the Norwegian colony. We hear that the settlers are satisfied with their new homes and our county. They work hard and have made great progress. They arrived late in the year, but started working at once and have kept going ever since, even after the snow came. They have built houses, roads, mills, etc. Several houses are finished since the winter started, and they will probably increase the settlement for new masses in the spring.

The schoolhouse is built by Carter Camp and they say the school is starting next Monday. A vapor saw and two water saws are established, and everything in the establishment is filled with energy and progress, something we can really appreciate. If these men are as hard-working farmers as craftsmen, it would not be long until the Ole Bull colony is the most prosperous in the county.

At the same time, articles critical of Ole Bull appeared in New York newspapers and in Norway. These accounts told of the colonists' disgust with the harsh winter weather and the late payments from Bull. His limited awareness of the colony's status and his unrealistic dreams for its development are reflected in this letter he sent to his brother, Edvard, from Georgia on Feb. 6, 1853.

Business, not indifference, but overwhelming business has delayed my answering your dear letter, and unfortunately my reply must be short, although I have so much on my heart that I long to tell you. Of my activity as an artist and a leader, and controller of my settlement in Pennsylvania, you can have a conception only when you know that I am engaged simultaneously in laying out five villages, and am contracting with the government for the casting of cannons, some ten thousand in all, for the fortresses, especially for those in California.

Philadelphia will subscribe two million dollars to the Sunbury and Erie Railroad, which goes near the colony to the south; New York has also given two million to a branch of the Erie and New York Railroad from Elmira to Oleana, the northern line of the colony, so that we shall be only twelve hours distant from New York, ten from Philadelphia, and about eleven from Baltimore.

So many people have asked for land that I have started looking for more. I have bought 20,000 acres to the west, and in the adjoining county (McKean) I have (the right of first) refusal of 112,000 acres. In Lycoming County I am contracting for an old, deserted iron factory with forests, water power, workshops, and dwellings, and am taking out patents in Washington for a new smelting furnace for cannons. For you this will be a perfect place, since you can be useful both for the colony, old Norway and your own family and old Ole.

You asked me how I could have got all this in operation, how I can, so to speak, play with millions. Good Edvard, when you see it for yourself you will be more surprised. This is merely a beginning. My knowledge has developed in proportion to the greatness of the project; my powers have grown proportionately with the magnitude of the work. My persecutors have themselves called into play my indisputable right to defend myself, and I answer with facts!

I am giving concerts every day, and must often go without my dinner, I am so driven. Today, Sunday, I have a moment free; tomorrow to Columbia and on to New Orleans; from there either to Washington, for the inauguration of President Pierce, or to California via Nicaragua; I will be back to visit the colony the end of April . . .

Bull never secured the additional property he mentioned in his letter. For that matter, he was in no position to afford more land. The scheme to manufacture thousands of cannons in Pennsylvania under contract with the federal government is a curious one, since the region lacked the iron ore necessary to supply such an endeavor. Most likely, some of Bull's friends with connections in Washington had led him to believe that they had the political clout to make the manufacturing facility and the rail links a reality.

Ole also announced plans to build a polytechnical school that would be staffed by European professors. It would function as both a civil and military institution open to youth across America. Teachers, craftsmen and laborers would be able to buy shares and supplement their salaries with dividends, according to a report that appeared in *Dwight's Journal of Music*, entitled "Ole Bull and his Colony," and authored by John Sullivan Dwight. West Point was seen as exclusive and aristocratic, whereas "the Oleana school would be for the people," Dwight reported.

He said Bull hoped to develop an efficient group of young men who would make improvements in weaponry and the national defense. Once the corps was trained, it would become part of the regular army. "Ole Bull's idea is tremendous," Dwight wrote. "We certainly need an institute as the one Ole Bull proposes for the people in general. He has shown enormous patience and energy, which makes him able to survive all hindrances. His scientific knowledge is stretching far further than pony tails and violins."

America was underdeveloped compared to Europe in its polytechnical education, so there may have been some merit in Bull's plan. However, he was too impractical and underfinanced to make it work.

Bull's absence created a leadership void that left even some of his supporters at Oleana feeling uneasy. A letter sent by colonist H. P. Olsen to a Christiania newspaper that February sounded the alarm, summarizing the opinions of many of the Norwegians:

There is nothing but big trees, high mountains, and narrow valleys; I have not seen such ugly land in Norway. So God help the poor Norwegians who come to Ole Bull's colony. Now we have all quit working, for no one has received as much as a penny for four months . . . We have appointed a committee to find Ole Bull or his companions, but so far they have not been successful. When those who are in Ole Bull's colony have received their money they will leave.

Elias Strangeland, an emigration agent whose recruiting services were rejected by Bull early on, waged a vigorous campaign against Oleana in early 1853. He maintained that land in the West was less expensive, more fertile and easier to cultivate. Strangeland was also the first to publicly question whether Bull held clear title to his Pennsylvania land.

Even Bull's own emigration agent, John Holfeldt, did an about-face. He declared in March that until he received additional information from Bull, he could not in good conscience advise emigrants to travel to Oleana.

Another blow was humorist Ditmar Meidell's ballad, "Oleana," published on March 5, 1853, in *Krydseren*. This attack on Bull's colony raised a roar of laughter in Norway and became the most celebrated song of Norwegian immigration. It reflected the conservative upper-bourgeois view of Bull's enterprise— that he was a dreamer who could not be expected to manage a serious business. However, the ballad was just as much an attack on the common people.

"Why the song hit," wrote Bjornstjerne Bjornson in *Norsk Folkeblad*, "was not just to make fun of Ole Bull, even though people thought he had made a fool on himself. The song described the establishment's thoughts of the labor movement."

A translated version follows:

OLEANA

I'm off to Oleana, I'm turning from my doorway,
No chains for me, I'll say good-bye to slavery in Norway.
Ole—Ole—Ole—oh! Oleana!
Ole—Ole—Ole—oh! Oleana!

THE OLE BULL COLONY

They give you land for nothing in jolly Oleana,
And grain comes leaping from the ground in floods of golden manna.

The grain it does the threshing, it pours into the sack, Sir,
You make a quart of whiskey from each one without expense, Sir

The crops they are gigantic, potatoes are immense, Sir,
You make a quart of whiskey from each one without expense, Sir.

And ale as strong and sweet as the best you've ever tasted,
It's running in the foamy creek, where most of it is wasted.

The salmon they are playing, and leaping in the brook, Sir,
They hop into your kettle, put the cover on, and cook, Sir.

And little roasted piggies, with manners quite demure, Sir,
They ask you, Will you have some ham? And then you say, Why, sure, Sir!

The cows are most obliging, their milk they put in pails, Sir,
They make your cheese and butter with a skill that never fails, Sir.

The bull he is the master, his calves he likes to boss, Sir,
He beats them when they loaf about, he's never at a loss, Sir.

The calves are very helpful, themselves they skin and kill, Sir,
They turn into a tasty roast before you drink your fill, Sir.

The hens lay eggs colossal, so big and round and fine, Sir,
The roosters act like eight-day clocks, they always tell the time, Sir.

And cakes come raining down, Sir, with chocolate frosting coated,
They're nice and rich and sweet, good Lord, you eat them till you're bloated.

Oleana

And all night long the sun shines, it always keeps a-glowing,
It gives you eyes just like a cat's, to see where you are going.

The moon is also beaming, it's always full, I vow, Sir,
A bottle for a telescope, I'm looking at it now, Sir.

Two dollars for carousing they give each day, and more, Sir,
For if you're good and lazy, they will even give you four, Sir.

Support your wife and kids? Why, the county pays for that, Sir,
You'd slap officials down and out if they should leave you flat, Sir.

And if you've any bastards, you're freed of their support, Sir,
As you can guess since I am spinning verses for your sport, Sir.

You walk about in velvet, with silver buttons bright, Sir,
You puff away at meerschaum pipes, your women pack them right, Sir.

The dear old ladies struggle, and sweat for us, and labor,
And if they're cross, they spank themselves, they do it as a favor.

And so we play the fiddle, and all of us are glad, Sir,
We dance a merry polka, boys, and that is not so bad, Sir.

I'm off to Oleana, to lead a life of pleasure,
A beggar here, a count out there, with riches in full measure.

I'm coming, Oleana, I've left my native doorway,
I've made my choice, I've said good-by to slavery in Norway.
Ole—Ole—Ole—oh! Oleana!
Ole—Ole—Ole—oh! Oleana!

"The ballad was what the romantic nationalists in Norway, who branded emigration as national desertion, wanted," wrote historian Theodore C. Blegen. "The song was chanted to the accompaniment of the folk laughter of a nation. But it was not the ballad that destroyed the hopes of Ole Bull and caused the colonists to go west. It was the inherent defects of the Utopia itself, ill chosen as to lands and weakened by dependence upon the bounty of the paternalistic and impractical Ole Bull."

Growing resentment toward Bull and disappointment is reflected in a letter colonist Jacob Olsen Wollaug sent from Coudersport on April 10, 1853. Arriving on the *Incognito*, Wollaug and family were persuaded by Bull and Holfeldt to travel to Oleana, where he would be paid $1.00 per day, or 50 cents per day plus free board:

"Everyone could select land to suit himself, from 25 to 50 acres, at $3.00 per acre to be paid for in three years at the rate of $2.00 per month. Bull was to furnish all necessaries, such as houses and the like, against a monthly reimbursement. Upon our arrival we found ourselves disappointed in our expectations, as the land looked very miserable to us . . . We found ourselves in the midst of high mountains and narrow valleys cut by small rivers, with heavy forest so that everyone understood that it would take a generation here to clear a farm or *gaard* that would adequately support a family."

Wollaug wrote that Bull visited the colony on Oct. 15, 1852. "We were then asked if we would work for a half-dollar a day without board. You can understand the effect of such an offer on the spirits of the colonists."

Supplies were expensive, despite the colony managers' assurances that they would be sold at cost, and families could not survive on 50 cents per day. After hearing the colonists' concerns, Bull agreed to adhere to the original terms and furnish work for the winter of 1852-53, leaving the Oleana settlers "free to buy land in the Spring, or not." Wollaug and at least one other colonist complained that Bull had vowed to return in eight days, but failed to do so, causing serious unrest.

"Bull remained away and no money came, until the people lost their patience, demanded payment for work already done, and stopped all future labor," he wrote. "John Cowan arrived back at Oleana in late February. He declared that Bull had not sent him money, but that in order to satisfy the people, he would pay us something out of his own pocket. I had to be content with 23 dollars; others received 15, yet others 10 and 5 on their accounts. I still have more than 50 dollars to my credit."

Wollaug was one of 16 Norwegian colonists fortunate enough to find employment in Coudersport as of April 1853. Even if Oleana left a sour taste in his mouth, Wollaug still supported emigration. In his letter, he wrote, "This much I have discovered: that the man who has strong arms, who can and will work, can earn a better livelihood here than in Norway."

Seemingly lost in the excitement and travails of the Oleana experience was Felicie. Her health was failing as she tended to the children. A letter from a neighbor written in March and April updated Ole:

As far as I know—and I see her every day—no one has heard her utter a word of complaint about anything. She knows herself that wounds can never heal when constantly torn open; they will grow shut only if left alone . . . She has been quiet, even reticent since she came out (of the hospital) and that may be easily understood, for she realizes to her sorrow that she has injured herself and her dear ones by many a rash word; but who has not done the same one way or another?

Last Sunday, March 10, she and the girls had dinner with us. In the afternoon some children came in, who danced and amused both us and themselves. An organ grinder happened to come along and for a short time he took my place in providing music for the children. It was a poor wandering Italian, who had his home and his family in Parma. The sound of his instrument coming up to us through a rear room affected her, it seemed to me, as the memory of one who was also wandering around without a home, and whose family now misses its support and provider.

She ought to get out in the air more. She went to church with me on the Sunday after she came back to the city and afterwards we went for a long walk, but lately she has not cared to go out walking. She loves to go driving with me. Her own horses and carriage— everything gone. She enjoys coming here to us and to Armin's and she has also been to Christian's a couple of times. She does not go any other place, except on special invitation. She has gained in weight during the short time, since she came to the city on the 19th of February.

When yesterday afternoon, Easter Sunday, we walked to "Lokken," Lucy was running back and forth like a little dog jumping around one and Felicie ran after her sister trying to catch her. Easter Monday, Felicie asked her mother if she might write to her Papa and she started to write a letter, which she finished today, but which is reposing in my desk. In spite of her zeal so many of the other children came around her, that she was interrupted every moment. More quiet would be necessary for this task, so Papa will have to take the will for the deed.

April 12: There are a number of vessels here, which are to leave during the week, some of them for New York with emigrants. Can these poor people find you? Are you able to fulfill the expectations which you have awakened in these hearts that are now struggling with doubt due to all of the contradictory information? Even our own employees, who have been in our service for many years, are departing with their families and their hard-earned savings. However, these people have had the intention of emigrating for some time— first it was to Texas, but the distance frightened them, their savings only being sufficient to take them to New York on the Zephyr, *one of Mons Thoresen's ships, which last year made the trip in 27 days. They are, however, equipped for 10 weeks and on their arrival at the point of destination a committee will be selected from the passengers, which is going to your colony to find out if it will be safe for others to go there.*

To be able to steel your wife against all unreliable rumors and newspaper statements it has been possible, in the meantime, to obtain such good news regarding your activity that it would give her some pleasure. I saw, for instance, a letter from one L.C. Prydtz dated Carter's Camp, Oct. 8, 1852, to his young wife, who with two little children was to join him in the Spring. It was filled with confident expectations. You had come onboard the ship yourself and had taken him and his traveling companions along. His sincerity appears through every word he writes to his wife. He is pleased with everything, he promises perseverance and hard work and expresses no doubt about anything. In a later letter he sends her a couple of gold pieces, telling her that this is the kind of money he makes there, and that he shall send her money for the voyage in a short time.

But one ship is being filled after another, and no money has been received by Mrs. Prydtz as yet. Do not think that I doubt that you will not do your best to help these poor people. But how much worry have you not had in the meantime, which may have broken down your courage and your strength? And then all these hordes of people that go from here!

Your treasurer, Mr. H., does not have a good name in this country. But I trust that with the help of God all wants have now been relieved with the proceeds of your concerts in the South and I do hope that Spring and Summer will bring us better news.

Your wife went along to inspect an apartment, for which the rent for the summer months was to be 70 specie dollars. We have dared to rent it without asking the custodian and I suppose this was wrong, but she did not want to ask him and a decision had to be taken at once if she and the children, who are coming here at the end of the month with Genevieve, were to find a place to live at this late date. The apartment is in the house of builder Malthe on Lower Voldgate around the corner from Christian's house, and it will be easier for her to take trips to the suburbs from there in the summertime without having to go through the city, which she does not like to do. Although the street is ugly, I think that the apartment will be very comfortable when it is fixed up, and because this is needed, it will be cheaper for the summer. Later on it will be 160 dollars per year. But that is a small matter. Education of the children will from now on cost more, so that in the future they shall be able to provide a good and comfortable home for their provider to rest in. And who could do this better than these blessed, loving souls, who are so tenderly attached to both their parents. They also have to go through their school, but it will only make them more lovable and more fitted to make both themselves and others happy— if it does not last too long and is of a harder nature than up to the present.

No matter how quietly and economically they live, it will be a different matter to make both ends meet in Christiania and a certain fixed amount for daily necessities, something that she could depend on for the children, would no doubt make your wife feel happier. I know that you will think about this, when you are able to do so, and please forgive me for mentioning it. No mention will be made of unnecessary items. A piano can be rented and walking is good and cheap. But how will your poor patience be able to plow through all this.

Interestingly, on April 24, *Morgenbladet* informed its readers that passengers on the *Zephyr* had abandoned their original plans to join the Oleana colony and others in Norway were changing their minds, as well.

Ole Bull, Maurice Strakosch and Adelina Patti continued their tour through the southern cities. Proceeds from one of the New Orleans performances were donated to two local orphanages. The group moved on to Chicago for three shows in April and then to Milwaukee. A concert scheduled for Buffalo after that was cancelled, reportedly due to an unidentified illness that struck Bull.

An article in the *New York Tribune* detailed the successful maple syruping operation and a plethora of deer, bears and trout to feed the residents as the colony grew. "Bull's colony in Pennsylvania is in a very satisfactory state of progress," the *Tribune* reported.

Although still ailing, Bull did insist upon returning to Oleana in time for the celebration of the Norwegian Constitution Day on May 17, 1853. This was the holiday he enjoyed more than any other; it's only natural that he would choose to observe it with his countrymen.

Few reports of the celebration emerged. However, many years later Potter County Judge A. J. Olmstead told journalist Torstein Jahr that he was among a group of about 50 local citizens who drove from Coudersport to Oleana for the affair. "Ole Bull was present and played on the fiddle," Olmstead said. "All kind of traditional Norwegian food and drink were served."

Bull's return after a six-month absence was a source of inspiration to the remaining colonists, perhaps reaffirming to some his continued commitment to make things work. Biographer Mortimer Smith wrote:

He plunged into the work of the little community, his mind teeming with elaborate plans. If any men of sound business sense were connected with the project, they must have surmised that disaster was not far off. But Ole Bull had not yet had to face the reality of the situation. His mind was still concerned with roseate pictures of the future, and the contagion of his enthusiasm must have affected his simple-minded countrymen who peopled the colony. Encouraged and inspired by the presence of their chieftan, the colonists during the summer months were full of hope and high spirits.

Another perspective on Bull's May 1853 return to Oleana is contained in this letter written by a colonist from Konsberg, who describes his "recruitment" by Bull and his eventual disillusionment.

I immediately got work in New York in my profession and kept my position until the great man, Ole Bull, arrived and told us that he had bought a large area which he intended to make into the New Norway where his fellow man could live in freedom and lead a better life than in the old country.

Nearly all of the Norwegians around here agreed on traveling there. I went one day up to Mr. Bull and asked him the conditions of the contract upon receiving us in his colony. Satisfied with what I heard, I left his house. Happy and delighted, I arrived home and told my wife about all the promises that this world famous man had told me and this also warmed her heart. We agreed that I should travel there alone until ev-

erything was in order and then she would follow.

About one week later I joined with others that made our way to Bull's colony. We were sure surprised upon arrival. We felt that we had arrived in a mountain village in Old Norway. All the plans that we had discussed on our way had now disappeared. My expectations were so great about the New Norway, but seeing what it really was took away my good mood and my courage.

Early the next morning, a portion of my traveling companions returned to New York, but I gathered my strength and decided to stay until Ole Bull arrived, so I could hear for myself his vision. I put the ax on my shoulder and walked to the forest to cut wood. This was the only kind of work that could be done. Not accustomed to this type of work, my fingers were soon raw and I found this kind of work was very difficult. But after two or three weeks my hands got used to it, as I got calluses. I now felt encouraged to cut the old growth pine trees.

I wasn't the worst of Bull's tree-cutters, among them a former shopkeeper, craftsman and old student who were partly troubled by large bellies, problems with their legs and other passed-down sicknesses that made it almost impossible for them to cut trees. It should be noted that the group was not only Norwegians, but people from all over Scandinavia.

After about a month, Mr. Bull arrived and said to us, "Isn't it beautiful here? Here we want to enjoy our lives. Let us make it comfortable for the people who come after us." But we didn't believe that. He was of the opinion that Norwegians could not live without mountains and rock. There were many among us who had traveled a good deal in America and told him how mistaken he was to buy this piece of land, when there were millions of acres of good land in America. He became angry and said that we did not understand what good land was. After this, he paid us and promised at our request that we would be paid monthly.

He was with us for some time and encouraged us with new promises. After a time, he left and promised to come back in a month, but Mr. Bull stayed away for a long time. It was October when he left and he did not come back until the 17th of May the following year. When he came back, there were not many left in his colony. We had almost all left during the winter.

I am waiting to see Bull come back and pay the people who are still in his colony, but this has still not happened. If he has forgotten or has no money, I do not know, but it is ugly negligence, for which he cannot be forgiven. Those people who are left are poor farmers from Gudbrandalen and Solor who are not able to get away from there on their own. We don't hear anything about Bull. God knows where he is, this poor soul who has lost lots of money from speculation. His loss is said to be about 70,000 dollars.

Nine

One of the mysteries of Oleana is the number of colonists who settled there. Other, smaller groups arrived after the *Incognito* passengers, including some Norwegian immigrants who relocated from southern states. Newspaper reports, eyewitness accounts and interviews with the colonists and their descendants are contradictory; tax records are incomplete or missing. Estimates range from 300 settlers to as many as 800. The true figure probably lies much closer to the lower figure.

Ironically, it was long after the colony began to unravel that Ole Bull officially became the property's owner. In May 1853, one month after Pennsylvania's General Assembly specially granted Ole Bull permission to engage in land transactions, John. F. Cowan and wife Rosetta deeded to Bull some 11 warrants of land in Stewardson and Abbott townships, totaling 11,144 acres. The price was $10,388. Cowan signed for receiving the money the same day. The deed was not recorded with Potter County until July 27. It clearly specified that three sections within the parcels, totaling 658 acres, were not part of the sale. Bull had immediate concerns about these deed reservations. Nevertheless, he pressed forward with his grand plans, evidently trusting that his aides would work out any discrepancies.

New Bergen on the north end of the colonial settlement bore some resemblance to a small village by July 1853. Several modest cottages of pine and hemlock had been neatly constructed, extending up a hillside to the east of the valley. Flagpoles visible from the road were adorned with the red, white and blue American flag waving in unison with the Norwegian banner of similar colors.

To the south, in Oleana, a new three-story hotel referred to as the "Lion Tent," complete with an adjoining dining hall that could accommodate 50 people, became the social center of the colony. Its owner and operator was Captain Louis Lowe, a Hungarian of the former Kossuth Guard. Lowe, in the Maygar language, means "lion."

A general store in the same vicinity had opened in early 1853. A painted sign in front of the building contained American and Norwegian bears in fond embrace, accompanied by the motto, "In Union There is Strength." Mounted atop the dining hall at the Lion Tent were the American, Danish, Hungarian and Norwegian flags. Also visible from the road, on a hillside opposite the hotel, was a flagpole carrying an unusual banner that blended the American and Norwegian patterns into one.

Ole Bull's cabin was now in place on the side of Nordjenskald Mountain, overlooking the New Norway settlement. Its location afforded a magnificent view of much of the surrounding country. The site could be reached by a path branching off from the road up to the crest of the mountain.

A log schoolhouse had also been built in the New Norway village, surrounded by about 15 cabins that were either completed or in the process of being built. Eleven children of Stewardson Township who had not been able to attend classes were welcomed into the Norwegians' school. The teacher there was Miss Beza Rook, originally from Jamestown, N.Y. There was also a school at Cartee Camp/New Bergen in Abbott Township. David Conway, son of a farmer in that area, was the teacher. One other educator, Otto Raas, a passenger on the *Incognito*, is associated with the Oleana colony.

The issue of education was a sensitive one, because Norwegian immigrants and religious leaders were generally critical of American schools and teachers. If Norwegian children attended the common schools, many feared, both the Lutheran faith and the Norwegian language could be lost. Furthermore, some pioneers believed that church and state ought to be linked, based on their own upbringing and education in their homeland.

Flowery—almost lyrical—prose continued to mark many of the newspaper stories about the colony's progress. Journalists did not feel obliged to limit their reports to verifiable fact, especially when the truth might get in the way of a good story or fail to advance the cause of a particular individual or group.

Anyone reading the exaggerated accounts from the *New York Tribune* in the summer of 1853 would have been convinced that Ole Bull's utopian vision was well on its way to fulfillment. The celebration of American independence on July 4 was to be based in a new 100' by 30' "grand concert hall" established as part of Bull's hillside "castle," the newspaper reported. The *Tribune* continued:

Ole Bull is certainly an extraordinary man. You can see him up at daylight in the morning, mounted on his impressive Norwegian horse, riding around examining his lands. After his breakfast you will see him assisting his workers at their labor, building his house. In the afternoon, he may be found working on the roads with quite a number of hands. The schools of the colony are flourishing and are under the care and instruction of teachers from New England. He visits them daily. When he executes a deed for any of his countrymen, he inserts a clause, depriving them of the privilege of selling liquors except for medicine.

A Potter County historian and writer, W. W. Thompson, discovered documents showing that even in the midst of financial problems and growing skepticism or disillusionment, Bull was plotting the development of a fifth village, to be called "New City." Its location, as far as Thompson could determine, was on the top or side of Nordjenskald Mountain. He reported:

It was never anything except on paper. In June 1853, a contract was entered into to build a road starting from a point near the lower end of the dugway near New Norway to intersect the chopping at New City and to be completed by July 4. No courses or distance given. From earlier correspondence we know that New City was to be on the top of the hill and that is all we know about it. The road was never built. The colony had commenced to disintegrate already and some had left.

As suddenly as Ole Bull had reappeared at Pennsylvania property, he vanished. Colonists were informed that his absence was due to illness and business commitments, but these explanations were unsettling. He would never again set foot in New Norway.

"It is with regret that we report that Ole Bull must stay inside his room in New York because of illness," the *People's Journal* reported on July 1, 1853. "We hope to see him well back together with us, since his appearance among his countrymen has so great influence. We think the sparkling water in Oleana and the strengthening air will be better for him than the atmosphere in New York."

Even without Bull's personal involvement, the Independence Day celebration of July 4, 1853, was a gala affair, attended by approximately 300 people. From New York, Bull sent back a large sum of money to be used for the purchase of fireworks and refreshments. Wild stories about the impending celebration had circulated in Potter County. There were rumors that Bull had purchased $7,000 worth of fireworks and supplied 12,000 bottles of wine. President Franklin Pierce was among the dignitaries reported to be planning a trip to Oleana for the festivities.

An afternoon feast at the Lion Tent was followed by a playful concert by two amateur fiddlers, with three prominent guests from Potter County acting as ceremonial conductors. They were: Lieutenant Colonel John M. Kilbourne, a hotel and sawmill operator who served in the Pennsylvania General Assembly; Frank L. Jones, who operated one of the first stores in Coudersport and doubled as Sheriff of Potter County; and William T. Jones, another prominent Coudersport businessman who had served as the town's postmaster.

Beer kegs were quickly drained, while wine and champagne also flowed freely. Later in the day, the Potter County guests were taken on a tour of the villages, then up the hill to Ole Bull's cabin.

As darkness descended, the women from the colony hosted a tea at the Lion Tent dining hall, with Louis Lowe as the master of ceremonies. With lightning flashing and thunder rolling, he called upon Coudersport attorney Crosby W. Ellis to offer remarks on behalf of the Norwegians. Ellis apologized for Ole Bull's absence and reminded those present that the purpose of the occasion was to celebrate the blessings of independence.

Hugh Young, a scribe from the *People's Journal*, reported on the evening's activities:

On the front of the Lion Tent were illuminated letters, "F.P." We asked what the initials meant and someone said, "Foolish People," which would be appropriate. We learned that they meant "Franklin Pierce." Now followed stars, rockets, Roman candles, telegraphs, etc., all on a grand scale. As the rockets going up met the lightning coming down, there seemed to be only one thing wanting to make this scene romantic— this was Ole Bull and his violin.

The fireworks over, the company again assembled in the ballroom, where dancing was again resumed until the rain drove them out; whereupon the Norwegians took their places, notwithstanding of rain and the unfinished condition of the ballroom, and danced beautifully. Then they sang the National Anthem of Norway and continued dancing until quite late.

At Andresen's, an accident occurred which, fortunately, resulted in no personal injury. Some of the gentlemen had retired to bed over the ballroom and whether from the crowded state of the bedroom or the shaking of the house from dancing, we are unable to say: but the effect was the breaking of a joist which let those in the bedroom down into the ballroom on very short notice. Those in the ballroom heard the cracking and made a precipitate retreat else the consequences might have been more serious.

Breakfast over, the parties began to disperse. And thus ended the Oleana celebration. We dispersed to think that the affair went off well. When we consider that this is a new colony and the great Norwegian was absent and sick, which made his countrymen feel anxiously uneasy, afraid that the anniversary was ours, not theirs; considering all these things, it went off very well. They were attached to Ole Bull and consider his sickness a colonial calamity. We hope for their sakes he will soon return and cheer them by his presence.

Adding to the colony's lore was another article from the *People's Journal* published a short time after the report on the celebration:

Cassius M. Clay from Kentucky has given Ole Bull a beautiful Durham bull calf that is ten months old and weighs 810 pounds, and an 18-month-old cow that is even bigger. The two healthy animals came to Oleana last Friday. This is joyful news because cropping will one day become a large industry in the county, and he who brings these animals to Oleana is a public benefactor. We are sure several of our citizens have good reason to thank Mr. Cassius M. Clay for his gift to the Norwegian chief.

Eyewitness accounts and family recollections provide valuable insight into what transpired at Oleana. These are, naturally, colored by the biases of the storytellers and subject to compromise by the passage of time. Nevertheless, they add color and a human dimension to the story.

Nellie Burt Maltby, the granddaughter of one colonial family, shared portions of her family's oral history during a newspaper interview at the age of 80 in 1965. A resident of Jersey Shore, she said her ancestors' experiences at Oleana were not unique:

The struggles of these pioneers to make a living among the mountains was rather unbelievable. It took two men a year to clear an acre. It was so dense and only small tools were available. The food available was cow cabbage, nettles, leeks and whatever fish and game could be caught. Other supplies were brought in by packhorse and most from as far away as Dansville, N. Y., or Jersey Shore, Pa. Flour was made in small band mills and stone ground. Bread was so dark some children would go into the corner of the schoolroom and eat, hoping they would not be seen by their schoolmates.

Some of the men had no socks, but wrapped their feet in rags for warmth. I've heard my mother say that when they went to school their mother would try to have one dress for each girl. There were five, counting two half-sisters. She would sit up nights washing and drying them by an open fireplace. It was an era of "do it yourself"— spinning, weaving, sewing, etc., if one could get the materials. My mother learned to knit socks at six years of age. Many of the things needed to carry on the every day existence were made by hand and hacked out of the forest, such as looms, milling equipment, vats for processing hides for clothing and shoes.

The suffering endured and the will to exist was really uppermost in their minds. Many of the settlers never knew why they had to leave the colony. Very few spoke English and, if they did, it was spiced with one word in Scandinavian, followed by English, and the Scandinavian could be Swedish, Danish or Norwegian.

Ole Bull was absent from the local picture much of the time and wild rumors spread among his own people. Of course, each family had its own ideas, some of which have been carried down to the third and fourth generations. Fires, floods and many things have taken all records away. The court records are few and sparse. The courts had not been well organized and many things did not require to be recorded and are lost to our present generation, much to our regret.

Ole Bull's prolonged absences from the Pennsylvania colony have been a source of speculation and skepticism for many years. Illness played a role; however, it's also possible that he was guilt-ridden and depressed, or that he feared repercussions from colonists who might feel betrayed or misled. Bull may also have been seeking to rectify the situation through negotiations or threats of litigation. There are even those who believe he simply lost interest.

Bull was not one to hold his emotions inside. One newspaper reporter quoted some of the colonists as stating that, when frustrated or perplexed, he would sometimes "take his violin and extemporize such wild, weird music as would sometimes make the listeners shiver."

Even in his absence, Bull was financially supporting the colony. This is revealed through documentation found many years later in the archives of the Riggs Bank in Washington, D.C. Bull was well-known in both the New York and Washington offices of Riggs Bank. Among the entries in the bank records is a $5,500 withdrawal on Aug. 4, 1853, "for workmen at New Bergen and Oleana," as well as a payment of $3,147 to John Holfeldt and several payments to John Hopper, one as high as $2,667. Bull also withdrew $209.30 to buy a white stallion.

What, if any, revenue the colonists could derive from agriculture was either poorly documented or not recorded at all. Bull might better have taken seriously a letter that Elling Larsen sent to him in August 1853. Recognizing the area's limitations for farming or mineral extraction, Larsen suggested that Bull consider the harvesting and processing of timber as a major income source.

"Even if the mountains were of silver and gold, truthfully they would be emptied as things are going," he wrote. ". . . Farming is safely one of the first, biggest and most indispensable for a colony as yours. But consider the great immense forest which in high degree surprises the farmer, yes which he hates and curses. No man in his life span is able to bring forth such a rich harvest as this God-made first and greatest harvest . . . The forest's turnover for money is one of the most important activities at the moment for your colony. And a few hundred dollars for machines of various kinds is enough to make (profits) from the simplest tree, the hemlock, to the better maple and cherry tree."

Larsen's letter also alluded to the fact that not all able-bodied settlers had been working while Bull was away, and he advised more careful recruitment of colonists: "To prevent such evils that hitherto have occurred an honest man should be sent to Norway because there he would be capable to judge if picked out persons are worthy to become settlers in your colony and thus there would not come any others than industrious and reliable people."

By the time Larsen penned his letter, Bull had recovered sufficiently from his illness to join Strakosch and Patti for their concert tour, beginning in New York and moving on to Boston.

Norwegians who were living in America were growing even more skeptical of Bull's plan. An article in *Emigranten* repeated concerns that the colony was too isolated due to the lack of rail transportation, while its soil was too rocky for farming:

Oleana has totally five houses, one occupied by the violinist, the second by Dr. Joerg's family, the third by a Danish family, the fourth by a Hungarian officer, and the fifth by Mr. Bull's horse. The colonists have already started to leave the colony. Ole Bull has been betrayed. It became apparent that he did not have any financial guaranty in the country; he had invested 250,000 dollars without getting anything back.

Elias Strangeland, the emigrant agent spurned by Bull in 1852, continued his attack on Oleana in this Norwegian newspaper account:

Elias Strangeland, who stayed in North America for four years, has returned to inform his fellow countrymen about the emigrated Norwegians' religious and civic conditions in the new country. Strangeland was previously a teacher in Karmesund. He will now help Norwegians to find cheap and secure transportation to New York and Quebec, and guide them how to avoid the American betrayers.

According to Strangeland, it is not the best solution for Norwegians to go to Ole Bull's colony, Oleana, because it has difficult land to farm. But on the other hand, we can not completely trust Strangeland on this point, because he, according to the American magazine Emigranten, *had given Ole Bull an offer to return to Norway to invite people back to America— an offer Bull refused. The* Emigrant *advises the Norwegians who plan to come to America not to listen to the suggestions from Tolke; either they spoke for or against the colony.*

Faerelandets Ven *has some advice and suggestions for emigrants, based on Strangeland's stories, a man the magazine trusts. They show this by printing several recommendations of him. On questions such as what part of America should one go to, Strangeland does not have any particular preferences. But he does not recommend Texas, Canada or Ole Bull's colony.*

He says this about Oleana, "The whole colonization plan, at least at this time, seems mysterious and risky, and not as prosperous as the western states, even though the transport is free from Norway. It is under doubt if Ole Bull is the owner of the colony, since he is referred to as an agent in America. People also look upon the project as a speculation, just to populate an empty piece of land."

No single event signals the unraveling of Ole Bull's colony. Its demise is poorly documented and most accounts of it are seriously distorted. Some who accepted Bull's invitation to build a better life in the Pennsylvania mountains were forever bitter. Other sympathized with Bull and their resentment was focused more on the freeloaders who barely lifted a finger to build the communities while others worked tirelessly to help fulfill the dream of their leader. The scattered reflections recorded for the ages by newspaper reporters, or passed down through the generations by word of mouth, lean more toward the former.

The one document that best symbolizes the colony's collapse can be found in the Potter County Recorder of Deeds office, dated Sept. 22, 1853. The deed conveys the property Bull purchased the previous year to John F. Cowan, with Bull receiving a refund of his $10,388 purchase price. Even that rather routine legal proceeding was the subject of a myth that Bull himself helped to create later in life. This outrageous tale appeared in Oddmund Vik's biographical book:

Weak from illness, he returned to his countrymen in New Norway. Then he realized how difficult it was. Stewardson, a Quaker, had several times tried to inform Bull about the situation in the colony. But Bull's ombudsman had been careful to keep away people who could wake Bull from the dream. But finally he managed. The Quaker was the proper owner of the property. Ole Bull was no longer standing on his own land, and it was as if he had sunken down in a boggy ground.

Suddenly, he threw himself on the horseback and started riding to Philadelphia. He had to speak to his managing clerk, the lawyer who was the middleman of the bargain. With his reputation, he had to protect his name against corruption.

There was nothing wrong with the papers; they were correct according to the lawyer. He offered Ole Bull some food, but suddenly Bull could not take anything. He only drank a cup of tea, even though he was both hungry and thirsty.

When Ole Bull asked the lawyer about Stewardson, he answered, "I have your money; the rest you must take care of yourself."

A few years later, the lawyer's sister told that the brother on his death bed had told her that he served Bull poison in the food.

The one shred of truth in Vik's account was the jarring discovery that many of the remaining settlers were, in effect, trespassing by occupying homes on property that neither they nor Ole Bull owned. They were given the option to purchase the land, but few could afford it.

This news was shared with readers of the *People's Journal*:

We understand the celebrated Norwegian, Ole Bull, has sold out all his interest in this county. He has no doubt discovered that although he can beat the world at playing on the fiddle, he is not capable of managing to advantage the colony which he had projected; or, perhaps, he finds he has not the time to give it his personal attention, without which it cannot prosper. Whatever the reason, he has sold out.

We trust men who will step into his tracks will now go to work and settle the land purchased of Ole Bull, with thorough going farmers. There is no better land in Northern Pennsylvania for farming purposes and all kind of produce are ready sale at enormous prices. For instance: Hay sold last winter within two miles of the colony to lumbermen for $15.00 per ton; oats for 60 cents per bushel; and other things in proportion. Any industrious, able-bodied man, desirous of purchasing wild lands in a good location will do well to make a visit to the Kettle Creek lands lately owned by the great Norwegian.

The news was also reported in the Oct. 12, 1853, edition of the *North American*, a newspaper in Philadelphia:

It makes us sad to hear that Ole Bull's colony is closed down. No more than 40 emigrants are left at the settlement, situated by Kettle Creek. It is known to have difficult soil, not suited for farming. Mr. Bull spent a lot of money on the establishment of the colony, built a beautiful hotel and other buildings, but a difficult lease made confusion, and became very expensive.

The mass exodus intensified, as families sought ways to abandon the mountain settlement before the onset of another winter. Some were able to afford the train fare to New York and sail back to Norway. Others relocated to Scandinavian settlements in Wisconsin and Minnesota. A few families also relocated to Iowa, Michigan and New York.

Louis Lowe from the Lion Tent, his temper flaring, sued Ole Bull and his agents. Lowe alleged that Bull had retained him as hotel manager for a salary of $60 per month and owed him $403 in back pay. When Lowe's collection efforts failed, the court ordered that Bull's violin be seized, despite his protestations that the instrument was an "indispensable tool." The *New York Tribune* editorialized that this was an act of "profanity" and asked its readers to imagine such an "ethereal creation" as Ole Bull's violin in the hands of a "barbaric deputy sheriff."

Another published account of questionable accuracy tells of some colonists, after being served eviction notices, storming up the mountain to Ole Bull's cabin, "denuding it of its fineries . . . The tapestries made dresses for the starving Norwegian women."

Bull was not abandoning his people. As late as October 1853, he was still sending money back to the disintegrating settlement as quickly as he earned it. An advertisement described the Nov. 2 and Nov. 4 concerts in Philadelphia as "for the benefit of the Oleana sufferers." Newspaper readers were informed that Bull would have to use a substitute violin, since his preferred instrument remained in the possession of the authorities.

A Philadelphia newspaper, the *Pennsylvanian*, on the eve of the first concert in the city wrote this exaggerated account:

Today is a test of whether the citizens of Philadelphia feel obliged to support Ole Bull in his mission to help the colonists. Five hundred people in the colony are about to die of hunger; the winter is approaching and they do not have anything to protect themselves from the hard realities.

Their protector has spent large amounts on Oleana. The mystery of this catastrophe is the reason why Ole Bull is asking for the audience's help. Let's help the suffering. The concert seems to bring in a large amount, because the tickets are selling fast.

An article in the Oct. 28, 1853 edition of the *New York Atlas* provides a glimpse of the public's perception, or at least the version that Bull would have wanted people to believe:

We learn that Ole Bull will give another concert for the relief of his settlers in Northern Pennsylvania, in Philadelphia, immediately after his concert in New York. It will be seen by the advertisement that the members of the colony are in a state of great distress and suffering. Ole Bull, with that forgetfulness of self and that humanity which has ever *distinguished him, has promptly come forward to minister to the relief of his suffering countrymen. Notwithstanding he has himself lost over $70,000 in this unfortunate affair, yet he no sooner hears of the distress of his countrymen than he forgets himself and his own wrongs and comes promptly to their relief. This is the noblest magnanimity and immeasurably transcends all the ordinary charitable appeals to which the New York public are ever so ready to respond.*

We venture to predict that the concert Ole Bull is about to give for the immediate relief of those poor, deluded, and suffering creatures will present one of the most crowded and enthusiastic audiences that the genius and the great musician himself has drawn together. Truly, "One touch of Nature makes the whole world kin."

Bull's own concerns about the colonists' plight are further demonstrated in a letter he wrote in early November while spending a night at the Arcade Hotel in Philadelphia. Apparently, Bull gave the letter to Robert Hamilton to hand-deliver to the remaining settlers when the surveyor brought them food, clothing and other supplies to help sustain them through the harsh winter.

"I have received accounts of the necessities of the colonists which have wrung my heart with sympathy, and made me keenly regret that these concerts were not still more productive," Bull wrote. "They would undoubtedly have been so but for the persevering efforts of the designing men who are endeavoring to sacrifice the colony and myself, and who reported elsewhere that there was no suffering at Oleana, and men caused statements to that effect to be issued in the public press. I intend to be at Oleana in a few days to renew the bonds of fraternity and good feeling which has ever united us, and which it is the hope of my life, can never be broken. Your faithful friend, Ole Bull." For whatever reason, Bull did not make his promised return.

One enterprising Potter County business concern saw an opportunity to exploit the colonists' troubles by taking advantage of the publicity Oleana had generated. A lumber company, Dodge and Brother of

Kettle Creek, wrote to the editor of the *New York Tribune* on Oct. 27, 1853:

When we have read that Ole Bull's colony has fallen down to the ground, we see the need to inform you that this is not the case, or then the people must blame themselves. There is more than enough work for the ones who want it. We are doing timberwork in the neighborhood of the colony, and need hard-working people. Several of the colonists are employed by us, and soon we can employ everyone who wants it.

This was likely a ploy to attract cheap labor for the rugged work of tree harvesting and lumber production in the Kettle Creek Valley. Bull's surveyor, Robert Hamilton, responded just days after the Dodge letter appeared in the *Tribune* with the following:

As Ole Bull's colony's surveyor, I will answer the letter from Dodge and Brother. I left the colony on October 4, and before I left I had a conversation with Dodge and Brother's agent, Mr. Herman Brown, who told me that they could not give labor to more people (they had six in their service). Several people are unemployed in Oleana; both men, women and children are hungry.

After the compromise between Cowan, Bailey and Longnecker was arranged to take care of the colony's debt, the transportation of groceries has been stopped. The horse that transported the food is taken away from them, and they are staying alive on the cost of private gifts.

Since I came to Philadelphia, I have been allowed to use the colonists' authorities to demand unpaid salaries (which has been impossible so far). Last week a source told me that they had to kill a bull and a cow Cassius M. Clay had given to Ole Bull, but it saved them from the death.

When I talked to the agent of Dodge and Brother, I asked him insistently to give more colonists work, but he said it was impossible. I feel it is necessary to give you this information because it is true, and when someone says that they do not suffer in Oleana, it is a big lie.

Robert Hamilton, Arcade Hotel, Philadelphia, Nov. 4, 1853

I agree with what Mr. Hamilton says. I know personally the facts myself.

C.W. Ellis, lawyer for the colonists

Bull and the other musicians moved directly to Washington, D.C., where they performed a concert for President Franklin Pierce and many members of his administration. Next stop was Louisville, by which time Ole Bull was publicly reflecting on his Oleana experiences, perhaps concerned that his image may be tarnished. Here are excerpts of an article appearing in the Dec. 6, 1853, edition of the *Louisville Times:*

Everyone has heard of the manner in which the renowned Ole Bull was swindled in his noble effort to plant a colony of his countrymen in the State of Pennsylvania. He who melted all hearts with the magic tones of his violin, found the feelings of the speculators flinty enough to beguile him into the loss of all his gains, and to render miserable and poverty-stricken those upon whom he expected and hoped to shower abundance and comfort.

With one of his energy, despair is never a welcome or an honored guest. That instrument, which had won for him a world-wide fame and had enabled him (had he been honestly dealt by) to realize the dreams long entertained, of conferring happiness and home upon his countrymen, by transferring them to this land of freedom, was again called into requisition. He is making a tour of the Union to procure supplies for the needy colonists who are suffering for the necessaries of life in this land of plenty, and who look for aid and comfort only to their great benefactor . . .

The recent pecuniary misfortunes of Ole Bull have created a sympathy everywhere, which has added vastly to his former popularity. His undertaking was praiseworthy in the first place— but truly noble is this last endeavor, to furnish food to the famishing, raiment to the scantily provided, and solace to the suffering. We know that he will be cordially greeted here where he and his able assistants are so warmly and highly regarded.

The trio rounded out its tour with stops in Chicago and then back in Philadelphia for the concert finale just after Christmas 1853. While Bull toured, additional families packed their belongings and headed toward Wisconsin and other westward points. Upwards of 50 colonists persisted in the Oleana communities to welcome the new year.

Bull biographer Mortimer Smith believes the colony's obituary could be written at the end of 1853. "The 'New Norway' that had been ushered in with such a blaze of glory little more than a year before, which had aroused so much interest in America and such high hopes among the peasants of the homeland— this New Norway had gone to join in limbo other American utopias," Smith wrote. "The colony founded by Ole Bull in poetic exasperation for the woes of his fellow Norwegians turned out to be a prescription worse than the disease."

Ten

Was Ole Bull swindled? Were his motivations as selfless and sincere as Bull and his supporters maintained? Was he the victim of his own naivete and unrealistic expectations?

These are among the questions that have lingered for a century and a half. Definitive answers remain elusive. The villains vary depending on who's telling the story.

The harshest judges argue that Bull's political ambitions combined with the greed of those around him led the colony's founders and managers to exploit the immigrants for cheap labor in clearing the land. However, few doubt the sincerity of Bull's commitment to the cause of preserving the Norwegian culture from outside infringements while giving his countrymen hope for a better life. Using his wealth and stature to rescue those people who wished to escape the enforced union with Sweden was a natural inclination for Bull.

Biographer Smith suggests that land agents induced Bull into purchasing the property by convincing him that the acreage was rich in mineral deposits. Smith refers to Bull's plan to insert a clause reserving mineral rights into each deed that conveyed land to the settlers.

"A land strongly reminiscent of home, a vague hint of possible mineral wealth— what better reasons than these could a man of Ole Bull's caliber require for the launching of a scheme that would intimidate the most practical and efficient of ordinary mortals?" Smith wrote. "He probably never gave a thought to the economic soundness of his scheme of colonization; in fact, he had very little scheme or plan but only the laudable, if extremely vague, desire to benefit his countrymen."

In contrast, Potter County historian W. W. Thompson suggested that Bull was anxious to raise his own financial standing. "The colony plan appealed to him from a standpoint of business— a chance to recoup the fortune he had recently lost in the National Theater, and a home and estate that would equal the lords of old Europe. The land could be bought cheap and sold cheap and, under the plan of selling only alternate lots at first, promised to be a financial and philanthropical success."

Spotty land records show that the property was initially acquired by William Penn and his heirs through treaties with the Indians. The Stewardsons, a Quaker family of Philadelphia, purchased vast acreage in southern Potter County in the 1790s. The owner of record until 1841 was Thomas Stewardson. Upon his death that year, the property was left in trust to Frederick Graff, the trust to run seven years after which the land was to be turned over to George Stewardson, a son, and William F. Vaux. They were designated as trustees to dispose of all property, comply with the provisions of the will, and divide the proceeds between four children.

John F. Cowan first appears in the records on Feb. 3, 1851, when trustees Vaux and Stewardson conveyed to him for a sum of $11,216 a substantial quantity of land scattered throughout southern Potter County. Even in the 1851 sale, some 10,995 acres were specifically reserved; that was a common practice of the times— keep the prime land and sell the remainder.

Bull's first entry in the official land records is through the colonial development company on which he was listed as president and financier. Cowan was superintendent and general manager. Joseph T. Bailey served as treasurer. Bull issued a series of notes to be discounted as needed to cover expenses of the colony.

It was not until May 24, 1853, some eight months after the colony's development had commenced, that John F. Cowan and his wife Rosetta deeded to Ole Bull for the sum of $10,388 eleven parcels of property in Stewardson and Abbott townships. These properties totaled 11,144 acres, about 5,000 in Abbott and 6,000 in Stewardson. In each transaction, the deeds defined three sections, consisting of 658 total acres, reserved for the original owners, Stewardson and Vaux, who had had nothing to do with the negotiations.

Almost immediately after the deeds were filed, Bull expressed concern about the wording. A letter sent to surveyor Robert Hamilton on May 25, 1853, read: "Mr. Cowan having sent a deed to me, according to promise, I see that some exceptions have been placed herein that somewhat puzzle me as I am not acquainted with the form in such deeds; therefore, I beg you to examine these carefully and explain matters to me."

Hamilton's reply, sent to Bull two days later, stated that much of the colony's construction occurred on property that Bull did not own: "One reservation will include New Norway and the garden and nursery grounds. The other will include New Bergen; also some three or four lots that have been selected and partially improved by the Norwegians."

Decades later, local historian W. W. Thompson investigated the land records and discovered that much of Hamilton's information was in error. Thompson reported that the reservations in the deed did not include the New Norway village, which by that time had upwards of 20 log cabins and the schoolhouse. His search showed that the reservations consisted primarily of a diagonal strip taking in much of the Kettle Creek valley and including New Bergen, Oleana, and the sawmill, nursery and garden areas of the Ole Bull colony. "Hamilton does not mention Oleana, which was certainly covered in the reservation," Thompson wrote. "If all of Ole Bull's information was no better than his surveyor's report, it is no wonder things went wrong."

The widening rift between Robert Hamilton and John F. Cowan is evident in correspondence Hamilton sent to Bull in July, marking the letter "confidential." In it, Hamilton warned Bull that Cowan may not be able to produce clear title to other massive land parcels he was trying to persuade Bull to purchase for continued expansion of his Pennsylvania domain. This included 25,000 acres north of New Bergen along Pine Creek and a 20,000-acre parcel located along Sinnemahoning Creek, far to the west of Bull's holdings.

Hamilton also warned of an alternative plot by Cowan to persuade Bull to abandon his Pennsylvania dream. Cowan would acquire the land at a reduced rate and then sell it to German investors who sought property in the region.

"Hamilton was not on good terms with Cowan at this time." Thompson wrote. "Bull had evidently bargained for a large amount of land with Cowan, either his own or that of some other person. It was for many years later not uncommon to give options on land with the idea of purchasing from the owner and pocketing the difference in price. Lands were cheap and speculation rife. Whether Bull had paid anything for his option, we are unable to state."

Bull apparently realized the extent of his predicament and, in July 1853, he turned to Wall Street attorney Lucius E. Bulkeley to bail him out.

Cowan, a shrewd and successful land agent, is a convenient scapegoat for those who want to believe that Ole Bull was bilked. However, any disputes or misunderstandings about the land ownership could also be attributed to sloppy land title searching, Bull's lack of business sense, as well as ineffective counsel.

Bull's sympathizers often fail to acknowledge the fact that Cowan did agree to refund the original purchase price. Additionally, Bull himself—in accepting that full refund—signed an affidavit specifically stating that he was *not* the victim of any skullduggery. According to one clause in that settlement document, "No fraud or impropriety shall hereafter be imputed to any of the said parties hereto. All charges of unfairness or imputation of dishonorable intention on the part of said John F. Cowan, Joseph G. Bailey and David Longnecker are removed by this letter."

That agreement, signed by Bull, Cowan, Bailey and Longnecker on

Sept. 22, 1853, spelled out the terms under which Bull would be repaid his $10,388 purchase price.

Did Bull sign the affidavit for expedience, recognizing that he could recover thousands of dollars by merely attaching his signature? It is difficult to believe that Ole Bull—frequently so apt to play the victim of others' indiscretions or insensitivities—would swear otherwise in writing the final chapter of an experience as widely known as Oleana. His earning power as a musician at that time was enormous. He could easily have earned the $10,000 in less than a year's time, without having to suffer the humiliation of signing a public document implying that the colony's failure was the result of his own neglect.

Although the circumstances under which Bull agreed to the statement will forever be a matter of speculation or conjecture, the settlement agreement stands as the one article of recorded history that, at least to a certain extent, vindicates John F. Cowan and his associates.

Even biographer Mortimer Smith, who as husband of Bull's granddaughter might tend to give him the benefit of the doubt, concluded that he was not defrauded.

There is no reason to believe that he was legally cheated by Cowan. That gentleman seems to have been a shrewd land speculator who always kept within the bounds of legal honesty, although there seems no reason to doubt that he misled Bull as to the value of the land in Potter County, or that Bull was the loser to the extent of many thousands of dollars, as he was the sole financial backer of the colonial company.

The Quaker Stewardson enters into the picture only as the owner of vast land adjoining Oleana. Hopper, for some years after the failure of the colony, pursued Bull with lawsuits for monies claimed as his legal advisor. For one who had been a bosom friend of Bull's on his first visit to America this was perhaps ungracious conduct, but his dire villainy was probably built up out of nothing more substantial than Bull's wounded feelings.

W.W. Thompson believes Bull, Cowan and others simply failed to do their homework before the immigrants set about developing their colony:

No doubt, Ole Bull's attorneys and agents knew of these reservations but, in the light of later developments, it is certain they did not realize just where the reservations were located. Otherwise, there would have been no settlement at New Bergen, Oleana or New Norway. In fact, the land would not have been bought had Bull known where the reservations were.

The records show that John F. Cowan and his wife had deeds for more than 50 tracts of land in Potter County between 1851 and 1853, containing from 50 acres to thousands of acres— one deed was for over 10,000 acres. In 1856, Cowan had 103 tracts of unseated land advertised for delinquent taxes in Potter County, most of the tracts full warrants.

No doubt through him Ole Bull did lose a lot of money, but if Ole Bull had been a businessman looking out for his own interests instead of trusting so much to others, it would have been to the interest of Cowan, with his immense holding of lands, to have cooperated with him.

It is evident that Cowan himself did not realize just where the reservations were located, or considered them of little importance, for he was part owner with Ole Bull in the sawmill property, was a member of the Ole Bull Colony Association, and did spend some time and money to promote the colony.

The colony was a losing venture, for all concerned with it must have lost. After the breaking up of the colony, Cowan did not settle the lands with Germans (as suggested in Hamilton's letter), but he did sell some of his land to William Radde, a New York German who settled in Germania in 1855, and Radde bought out some 15 colonists who had remained, they moving to the west . . .

John F. Cowan was a very prominent and wealthy man in Pennsylvania. If the swindle of lands had been anything like what has been gen-

erally reported, there is no reason why Ole Bull could not have made him reimburse. It is nonsense to talk about legal costs and the like. Any man who could with his violin and bow earn from $500 to $1,000 every night he was willing to face an audience had the best legal talent in the United States at his call, and could laugh at court expenses. No suit in connection with the land deal was instituted.

The facts appear that Ole Bull had been deceived and had deceived himself. Had it been a thing he could have carried through before his enthusiasm had a chance to cool, he would have stayed with it. As it was, he was simply compelled to drop the matter as he had others.

Many years after Thompson's summaries appeared, Norman B. Wilkinson, an assistant state historian for Pennsylvania, studied Ole Bull's experiences and concluded that Cowan "successfully perpetrated a sharp practice not uncommon among speculators in Pennsylvania lands." Wilkinson, in a 1953 essay, contended that Cowan represented himself as having authority to convey the property, then sought to buy it himself at a lower figure from the Stewardson estate.

"Unfortunately for Cowan—and Bull—Stewardson was not inclined to sell at the price offered," Wilkinson continued. "Obviously, Cowan had never been able to give Bull a clear title, but whatever instrument of conveyance had changed hands, or had been promised, it had been trustingly accepted without careful inspection. A defender of Cowan has declared that the deeds given him did contain conditions and limitations to which he did not pay sufficient attention. Bull's knowledge of the English language was indeed scant, but it should be assumed that if his American associates had been men of integrity they would have counseled him on such matters."

Another take on the issue was provided by Samuel Haven Glassmire, in a story he wrote for the Aug. 11, 1920, edition of the *Potter County Journal*. Glassmire was disturbed that certain historians had belittled the efforts of Ole Bull and ruled out any possibility that Bull had been cheated. He wrote:

It must be remembered that a fraud and swindle could be, and actually was, perpetrated on Ole Bull. Call it by the name of "reservations" or "bad title," as one prefers. The facts are that Ole Bull innocently believed that he had good title to about 11,000 acres of land in a body along Kettle Creek Valley and he naturally located his settlements and built his improvements on the very most favorable locations, which, as it afterwards developed, had been "reserved" in his deeds without his knowledge, leaving him the mountain sides and no title at all to the very land on which New Bergen and Oleana were erected.

It is idle to say that Ole Bull should have read his deeds and known. It is much more like simple justice to admit that Ole Bull, then a simple foreigner, was imposed upon and defrauded (in the name of "reservations") out of his choicest possessions. When he at last discovered the fraud (for such it was), he was heartbroken and discouraged and had he not been deceived in the purchase, the colony in all probabilities would have been prosperous and successful instead of a tragic failure.

A lengthy letter dated Nov. 18, 1853, from Bull's Wall Street attorney, L. E. Bulkeley, printed in the *New York Herald* as well as several magazines is worthy of consideration for both its historic value and its summation of Bull's "official" position on the issue:

Mr. Editor, I read a letter about Ole Bull's colony in your paper the 16th, and it is my duty as Bull's accountant (when he is away from town) to alter the impression the letter could have on the audience, since almost none of the paragraphs have reference to reality. It seems like the author of the letter is Yorg (Joerg), a medicine man who came from the west and lived for free in one of Ole Bull's houses. But as he gave the impression that he was a friend of Ole Bull and the Norwegians, he has in secret sworn to drive away the Norwegians and settle the colony with Germans, his own nationality.

He tried to get the position as supervisor without any luck. His be-

havior in the colony has been marked with stupidity, and he has never accomplished anything except for bringing a man to the colony who apparently is the same kind of wolf as himself. It is clear who this letter stems from, and that he wrote it in order to fit certain persons' views. In the name of justice, I require a complete description of Ole Bull's unhappy connection with this person.

In the summer of 1852, John F. Cowan from Williamsport and Joseph T. Bailey from Philadelphia and others were introduced to Ole Bull through this man who then was his lawyer. They persuaded him to give up his plan he had almost finished to buy land in Virginia and establish a new colony in Potter County. They blackmailed Ole Bull for $1,500 to visit the place. A person close to the deal, whose name I will not mention, had fooled a farmer who lived in the neighborhood to say to Ole Bull that the land was worth $5.00 per acre and the price was increasing.

Mr. Cowan, the company's leader, got Mr. Bull and Mr. Dudley to believe that 20,000 acres—and the only flat land—belonged to him. That was the way he convinced Mr. Bull to found the colony in that area. A large sum of money was immediately paid by Mr. Bull to send emigrants over to America. Later, a meeting was arranged in Philadelphia while Mr. Bull was away. Mr. Cowan was appointed superintendent and manager, Bailey cashier and Mr. Bull president.

Cowan got $10,000 from Mr. Bull without any compensation, not even a receipt. Bailey got $25,000 from Bull through Cowan and another guy. It is said they were supposed to give Mr. Bull a deed, but Mr. Bull never got a written proof.

Ten months after Cowan got the money he had to post a deed for 10,000 acres, which meant that he in secret gave away the land that was the reason why Mr. Bull agreed on the deal. This corruption was not uncovered until I became Mr. Bull's lawyer and traveled to the area myself. I then realized that neither Bailey nor Cowan had ever owned the land. Everything belonged to Mr. George Stewardson in Philadelphia. The two men had several times approached Mr. Stewardson in *order to buy the land, but with no luck. Mr. Bull had paid $20,000 out of his own pocket to build houses and to help settlers who said Cowan never paid for their work.*

Bailey kept the $25,000, and Mr. Bull never got any deed. When he finally asked to get money back or a deed, the only answer he got was that he was a foreigner, and could therefore not own land. I have heard Bailey is known to be a swindler, but the fact that he (learned) that Mr. Bull was a foreigner only after he got his money is not a compliment to his historical knowledge.

I was hired as Mr. Bull's legal advisor in July, and when I understood the terrible condition of his matters, I advised him to let go of everything and demand to get the money back. After almost three months, which is how long it took to get the legal papers in Potter County and other places, a compromise was settled between the partners. Mr. Bull passed the deed to Cowan and got his first $10,000 back in monthly payments. He withdrew from the company with a personal loss of $40,000.

After this meeting, Mr. Bull took hand of part of the company's debt, and we are paying it back as soon as we are getting in touch with the different persons. Bailey and Cowan agreed to pay the rest of the debt, but have not done it yet. It is this non-fulfillment that has caused all the troubles in the settlement, and made Mr. Bull the target for lots of criticism.

The attempt to give Mr. Bull all the responsibility for the non-fulfillment in the colony is typical for Bailey and Cowan. The trouble is to be blamed on them; as managers and cashiers, they have responsibility for the colony's mismanagement. Mr. Bull was not aware that the people on this land were fooled by these two men to buy it for $1.00 and $1.50 per acre, while people in neighborhood in Philadelphia paid 25 cents to 75 cents for better land.

The swindler wrote in a letter that Mr. Bull had not lost any money in his dealing with the company, that he sold it for double the price of what he bought it for, and that they only had pleasant negotiations— Mr. Bull and the landowners. He knew that every word was untrue.

Ole Bull is not a businessman, that is a fact, but to claim that he is not philanthropic is totally wrong. His actions tell the true story.
L.E. Bulkeley, Nov. 18, 1853

Torstein Jahr puts a great deal of stock in the Bulkeley letter. "As far as I know, no one has tried to argue against him. It seems to be the last word in American newspapers about the Ole Bull colony." Jahr's interviews, research and analysis led him to this conclusion:

Ole Bull got defeated, and lost lots of money. As he wrote to his wife at another occasion, "Too much need for me to help other people in need made me forget that I myself need." That is part of the reason why it went wrong.

But the part of his character that Jonas Lie calls "his economical misjudgment" would always have been an aspect, even if he did not meet the swindlers. He was known as being naïve, impractical, and not a businessman. Such a reputation is unpopular in America. The Oleana affair made him some enemies, but close friends supported him. He was still the same great artist and humanitarian.

Perhaps the version of events detailed in his widow Sara Bull's 1882 book represents Ole's personal or preferred description of the colony's demise. Its thoroughness and accuracy are suspect, but it is revealing in its own right:

He was now (March 1853), in his broken state of health, to make a crushing discovery. He found that the title to the land in Pennsylvania, bought and paid for by him in full, was fraudulent, and that even the improvements he had made were a trespass on another man's property. The forests were cleared, and 800 settlers had already made their homes there. Mr. Stewardson, a Quaker, and the rightful owner of the land, had for a long time tried to reach Ole Bull by messenger and letter; but his efforts had all been futile, so carefully had Ole Bull's business agent watched the mail, always sent to his care, and guarded him from approach.

When at last the artist, on his return to Pennsylvania, was legally notified that he was trespassing, he was dumbfounded. He mounted his fine saddle-horse and, without rest, rode to Philadelphia to see his lawyer and agent who had made the conveyance, hoping that this man's good standing in his profession, the church, and society, was a guarantee for fair and honest dealing.

The latter tried to quiet his client by telling him that his papers were good, and insisted that he should eat something before they talked more about the matter. Seated at the table, Ole Bull felt a sudden aversion to the food, although faint from his long fast and ride, and he refused to eat or to drink even a cup of tea. At last the man, when faced by the desperately excited artist, who insisted upon his going with him to the claimant, Mr. Stewardson, if the papers were right, suddenly changed his bearing, and taunted Ole Bull with his inability to do anything to help himself, saying: "I have your money; now, do your worst!"

The sister of this man met Ole Bull some years later, and told him that on her brother's death bed he confessed to her that he had poisoned the food and cup of tea that he tried to persuade his client to take, and to which he had felt so strange an aversion.

Mr. Stewardson was interested in Ole Bull's efforts to found his colony, and offered to make a sale of the land at a very low price; but the artist was able only to buy enough land to protect the people already settled there, and secure the improvements. He brought a suit against the swindlers, who now became his malignant and relentless persecutors. They tried to cripple him in every way; to prevent his concerts by arrests, and, having acted as his counsel, they were in possession of his papers and valuables, which they claimed for services rendered him, and attached his violin again and again for debt.

While on a trip in the Western States, he was exposed to malarial influences along the Mississippi, and the illness which followed proved the most serious physical ailment he had ever suffered. He was finally prostrated by chills and fever, was abandoned by his manager, and later taken to a farm-house on a prairie in Illinois, the hotel-keeper fearing to keep him, lest the disease should prove to be smallpox. He was so ill that he was delirious. As soon as he partially recovered his strength, he resumed his concerts, but the proceeds of these were swallowed up by the expense of his suit in Pennsylvania, and by the security he was often forced to give to release his violin from the attachments put upon it by his persecutors.

With untiring energy, though his health was much broken by fever and overwork, he persevered with his lawsuits and succeeded at last in wresting some thousands of dollars from the man who had swindled him. Five hard, struggling years were spent in this way. The help and succor he received, as often before, seemed Providential.

Two decades before Ole Bull and the other Norwegians set foot in Potter County, an essay entitled "Opportunities for Immigrants in Western Pennsylvania," by John A. Roebling of Butler County, Pa., was widely circulated throughout Europe. This 1832 essay contained words of warning that Bull might better have heeded:

One reason for the fact that large sections of good, fertile land in the most cultivated state in the Union have lain waste for such a long time is that there was too much wholesale trading carried on with these lands and thereby the titles and legal rights became confused, and much fraud resulted. Many a person bought land from someone whose right of possession was not established. Ignorant, credulous immigrants who were unfamiliar with the language here easily became the victims of such fraud. Great caution is necessary in buying land here in Pennsylvania.

Eleven

The identities of some of those who followed Ole Bull into the wilds of Pennsylvania will never be known. A handful remained in Potter County after the colony's demise to accomplish the purpose for which they had come. Several went on to distinguish themselves in commercial and governmental affairs. Here's a summary of those whose paths could be traced:

SUCKOW FAMILY

One of Ole Bull's managers and/or secretaries at Oleana was Bertol W. Suckow. A native of Bergen, Suckow and his Danish wife, the former Caroline Marie Knoblauch, came to America in 1846. Suckow was working as a bookbinder with the American Bible Company in New York City when he renewed acquaintances with Ole Bull, whom he knew in Bergen.

Suckow, his wife and their four-year-old son, Ludwig, came to the colony with the *Incognito* group in late 1852. Their daughter, Caroline, was evidently the first Norwegian girl born in Oleana.

After the failure of the Oleana colony, Suckow went back to New York and from there went west to Rock Prairie, Wisc., in 1854, where he became the bookbinder for the Scandinavian Press Association. This organization, which had been started by the Norwegian ministers in Wisconsin, had set up a small printing plant at Inmansville in the Rock

Prairie settlement, and begun publishing a newspaper, *Emigranten*, some years before.

Suckow later operated his own bookbinder company in the Wisconsin cities of Beloit and Madison, publishing *Picture Magazine* in the latter. He ended up in Milwaukee, where he died in 1885. His widow married Samuel Claussen, a grain merchant and mayor of Clear Lake, Iowa.

SOLBERG FAMILY

Olaus Solberg, a Norwegian baker who moved to Soro, Denmark, brought his family to America in 1853 in hopes of improving his economic condition. Among those arriving was his son, 20-year-old Carl Fredrik Solberg, as well as C. F. Solberg's stepmother, sister and an adopted child.

C. F. Solberg had recently graduated from a select school in Denmark and would become a prominent journalist in America. During an interview with a Milwaukee newspaper reporter in July 1919, he shared some vivid memories of his brief stay in the Pennsylvania mountains.

He recalled that after the family arrived in New York, his father, 40 at the time, had been persuaded by Ole Bull to move to the Oleana settlement and help manage the colony.

"Most of the settlers were very poor and were then building small loghouses and trying to clear farms in the stony mountainsides of Ole Bull's ridiculous purchase," Solberg told the reporter. "The colonists had a hard time of it. What induced Ole Bull to buy this miserable mountain tract when millions of fertile acres were to be had in the west is hard to say, unless he had some fantastic idea that the settlers would feel more at home among mountains, as in their own native land. At any rate, he was shamelessly swindled and his dream of founding a little Norway in America was soon to fall through. The 'New Norway,' as much as it could be called so, was to spring up in the west, beginning in Illinois and Wisconsin. Two or three good-sized and more comfortable houses were built at Oleana, one being intended for Ole Bull when he should be there, and one for our family."

Solberg spoke with pride and a certain amount of arrogance about his education at the academy in Denmark and the cultural differences he encountered at Oleana:

"It was a school for sons of the nobility and the rich . . . In addition to book studies, we were taught every accomplishment then thought necessary to a gentleman. We had our own botanical gardens, swimming and skating pools, riding grounds and the like, and received instruction in music, horsemanship, dancing and social deportment as well as intellectual training. We were also taught English, German and French, and as I thus knew English before coming to America I had an advantage over many other immigrants.

"After I had been in Oleana a few days I found that my fine clothes were out of place. I couldn't wear polished shoes and kid gloves in a lumber camp and do anything. This gave me much anxiety, but after about three weeks I had my mind made up and went to my mother and told her I was going to discard my broadcloth for a leather suit and logger's boots. She felt badly at this resolution, but there was nothing else to be done. Very soon I became a regular lumberjack and cut down trees and floated them down the rivers with the rest of the men and had my share of falls in the icy water.

"As there was no way for most of the settlers to make a living at Oleana, they had to go out and work in camps and factories and on distant farms of other settlers, and I soon decided to leave, too. I went about 90 miles down the river valley and obtained employment with a farmer named Goodman. When he learned that I was a newcomer and city-bred, he said good-naturedly, 'Well, Fred, we'll try you first on splitting kindling and see how you get along,' and he took me out to the woodpile and left me.

"After I had been working a while a servant girl came out of the house with two pails. These she threw at me and told me to bring her some water from the spring some distance below and went back into the house. I couldn't help smiling at myself. I had never been accustomed to such treatment. 'You surely are a gentleman no longer,' I thought, 'to be cuffed around by a servant girl.' After I had recovered from my astonishment, I brought her the water and was then ordered by her to bring in the wood. She gave me to understand that I was to wait on her. I got along well with my employer, however, and stayed with him a long time."

The fact that C. F. Solberg crossed paths with Bertol W. Suckow at Oleana was one of mere chance, but it proved to be a key encounter.

"The paper was in need of an editor and, as Suckow knew that I had some education, he urged the owners to try to engage me," Solberg told the Milwaukee journalist in 1919. "I was induced to come west. I had been doing farm and other rough work all this time and had just about arranged to go with a party of four other young men on a long prospecting journey among the eastern mountains and was somewhat reluctant to give this up. We had expected to be away about three years. When I had finally agreed to change my plan, arrangements were made to have me conduct an immigrant family of one Jens Jacobsen on their way west, which I did. It took us a week to make the trip."

Solberg became editor of *Emigranten* in June 1856. A year later, the newspaper was relocated to the booming city of Madison, where Solberg would become outspoken about the social and political issues of the day. The Republican Party was becoming a political force and slavery was a major topic of debate at the time.

"Our paper *Emigranten* called itself an independent democratic paper, but we were decidedly anti-slavery and Republican in spirit," Solberg recalled. "This was distasteful to some of the Democratic politicians, both inside and outside the nationality, and so the Scandinavian Democratic Press Association was organized by them and a rival paper (*Nordstjernen*) started . . . When the new Norwegian paper was started I became at once one of the targets of its abuse. We had it hot back and forth, but I felt that I had the better of it as our paper was on the right side of public questions."

Eventually, the rivalries faded and *Emigranten* devoted itself to broad discussions of the issues of the day. Solberg did cross paths once again with Ole Bull a short time after he became editor.

"It was during my first year in Madison, 1857, that Ole Bull made his first visit to that city," Solberg said. "Wisconsin at that time had the greater number of Norwegians then in America. He stayed a couple of days in Madison and gave two concerts in the Baptist church, about the first of July. We entertained him as best we could and he did me the honor to visit me in my office on the third floor of our quarters at the corner of King and Webster streets, where *Emigranten* was then published. I remember when he came he took the stairs two at a bound."

C. F. Solberg's comments suggest a motivation for Bull's founding of Oleana that is at least worthy of consideration. "Mr. Solberg thought Ole Bull had political ambitions," wrote Torstein Jahr. "(Solberg said) that Bull wished to become a congressman and that had something to do with the colony."

Bull was known to admire the U.S. system of government and had developed at least cordial relationships, if not political alliances, with some federal lawmakers. His grand aspirations for thousands of Norwegians to populate his northcentral Pennsylvania lands would have given him a natural constituency for establishment of a congressional district and his election to the U. S. House of Representatives.

In 1860, Solberg directed the first merger in the history of the Norwegian-American press by buying *Emigranten* and *Nordstjernen* and consolidating them under the former's name. During the first years of the Civil War, *Emigranten* was practically the only Norwegian paper in the nation. The newspaper strongly supported abolition and the candidacy of Abraham Lincoln, and Solberg took pride in Wisconsin's strong partisanship to Lincoln in the 1860 election.

Solberg became well acquainted with governors and other influential politicians over the years. He became a force for prison reform, recognition of Norwegians' contributions to the Civil War and other popular causes. While one-eighth of "original" Americans volunteered, as many as one-sixth of Norwegian immigrants joined the service.

His father, Olaus Solberg, was one of the pioneer settlers of Freeborn County, Minn. With the political influence of his son, the elder Solberg was able to join the 15th Wisconsin Volunteer Infantry, the so-called "Scandinavian Regiment," even though he resided in Minnesota.

When this group went south to St. Louis, C. F. Solberg rode along and sent letters to his newspaper concerning the regiment and other military matters. Solberg was also instrumental in organizing separate factions of the Lutheran congregation in Wisconsin. As the anti-slavery struggle grew in intensity, *Emigranten* was largely used as an organ by Lutheran ministers to lobby for abolition.

After the war, a new Norwegian paper called *Fædrelandet* was started at La Crosse. Solberg sold his newspaper to that publisher and relocated to La Crosse to assist in the consolidation. In 1870, he moved to St. Paul, where he established another Norwegian paper, the *Minnesotan.* Soon afterward, he sold that business and was appointed assistant secretary of state and state statistician. Later in life, he became involved in railway office and insurance work, eventually moving to Milwaukee.

Solberg married Laura Oppegaard from Rotnes in Nicollet, Colo., on July 17, 1872. They had three children. Olaus Solberg moved to Watonwan, Colo. He died in Mankoto, Minnesota, in 1907 at the age of 95.

ANDRESEN FAMILY

John Henry Andresen, known more commonly as Henry Andresen, a native of Denmark, was hired by Ole Bull in New York City to serve as secretary and clerk of his Pennsylvania colony, beginning in 1852.

He would eventually purchase much of the property that comprises the Oleana village of today and remain in the area for the rest of his life. An intelligent and enterprising man, Andresen was able to read and write in seven different languages. He could also add, subtract, multiply and divide columns of figures with great speed and accuracy.

In 1856, Andresen took over the log store and hotel at Oleana from owner Julius Johnson and would continue to operate the business until 1880, when his adopted son, Willard Andresen, became the owner. Henry

Andresen was responsible for many of the early improvements in Stewardson Township. In 1856, he opened a gristmill. Later, he started two sawmills, one at the junction of Little Kettle Creek and the main branch of Kettle Creek, and the other farther downstream on Kettle Creek, just north of today's village of Cross Fork. Andresen was the first of the colonists to become a U.S. citizen, receiving his papers on Sept. 22, 1857.

Potter County tax records of 1869 listed Andresen as a miller, lumberman and dealer of merchandise. He was also postmaster at the Kettle Creek Post Office, as it was called at the time, in Oleana. Additionally, Henry Andresen became the town clerk.

Shortly after Andresen's arrival in Oleana, he met his future wife. Mary French was not at all typical of the women of her era. In 1843, she and her husband, Francis D. French, opened a house for travelers alongside the turnpike, just north of Oleana. Their large home also served as the local post office and was used for religious services.

Mary French had enjoyed hunting and trapping with her husband. She was particularly adept at hunting wolves that roamed the region in the 1800s. Deer, elk, bears and cougars were also among her quarry. When a lumber company sought employees to help drive logs down Kettle Creek, Mary French stepped right in alongside the men.

After the death of Francis D. French in 1850, Mary took a job as a cook at the Lion Tent where, according to a newspaper report, she was not at all charmed by the behavior of the guests, with the exception of Henry Andresen. "She says they danced and carried on too high for her," the *Potter County Journal* reported in its Nov. 17, 1897, edition. "Many a time, she declares, the Norwegians would dance all night to the tune of a squeaky fiddle, instead of resting for their day's work clearing new ground for their little farms."

Not long after her marriage to Henry Andresen, the couple adopted a boy, Willard Colkin, who became Willard Andresen. Later, Mary became involved in his business affairs, including a financial interest in *The Potter Enterprise*, a weekly newspaper founded in 1874.

Financial problems forced Henry Andresen to sell about 6,000 acres to Coudersport businessman Frank W. Knox in 1877. Andresen died at his Oleana home on Feb. 4, 1890. Mary Andresen died a few years later. Willard Andresen moved to Colorado and operated a farm there sometime during the 1890s. He eventually returned to Oleana and continued farming.

JOERG FAMILY

Born in Leipzig, Germany, in 1808, Dr. Edward Joerg was the son of a prominent gynecologist. He conducted studies of childhood diseases, a career that took him to England, France and the United States. Joerg was called to Havana, Cuba, in 1838 as part of an international effort to discover the germ that caused yellow fever. He became manager of the hospital in San Carlos. It was there that Dr. Joerg met Maria Agatha Belot, daughter of the French doctor, Charles Belot, who operated a hospital in Cuba.

Joerg's connection with Ole Bull dates back to 1843. Maria, an accomplished pianist, played accompaniment for Bull when the latter visited Cuba that year. Bull was a guest of Dr. and Mrs. Joerg during his stay in Cuba. They chose him as the godfather of their oldest daughter, Louise.

The Joergs relocated to a German farming settlement in Illinois, not far from St. Louis, Missouri. In 1852, Ole Bull visited them in Illinois and apparently persuaded Edward Joerg to relocate to Potter County and operate a hospital that the musician planned to develop there.

The way Dr. Joerg would later describe things, he and Mrs. Joerg and their six children arrived in 1853 to discover that the facility was nothing more than an unfinished log cabin and the colony was already beginning to unravel. Nevertheless, the Joergs planted their roots in Potter County and remained.

Through an arrangement with John F. Cowan, the Joergs purchased about 1,000 acres of forestland in Stewardson Township, in the vicinity of the vaguely-defined village of Valhalla envisioned by Ole Bull. As might be expected, the transaction included certain reservations. Cowan reserved the rights to one-acre lots surrounding each building within the parcel, with the exception of the Joergs' own home.

The Joergs' seventh child, a son named Herman, was born in 1854. Shortly thereafter, the family relocated to Coudersport so their children could attend school there. Dr. Joerg also opened a medical practice in Coudersport. At the same time, he contracted with local builders for the construction of a large dwelling along the road near today's Ole Bull State Park. Huge stones were pulled from the bed of Kettle Creek by a yoke of oxen to build the walls of the home. The Joergs also purchased a portion of the reserved property from Cowan, including the mountain shelf that contained Ole Bull's home site. Carved wood from Bull's abandoned cabin was used in the construction of the home.

Dr. Joerg practiced medicine in Coudersport until 1864, when his family moved into the stone house, where he died from diphtheria on August 17, 1866. His funeral was held at the home of Pierre A. Stebbins on East Second Street, an apartment house now known as The Five Elms along Ludwig Lane. His was the first Masonic funeral held in Coudersport. Maria Joerg and the children remained involved in the Coudersport community. Their son was appointed Coudersport Postmaster while maintaining a farm south of Oleana.

On June 1, 1895, the Joerg family sold their forest land to Lackawanna Lumber Company for $28,000. Maria Joerg died in October 1908.

The former Joerg home near Ole Bull State Park was occupied by a state forest ranger when it was destroyed by fire on March 8, 1925. It was rebuilt and continued to be used as the ranger's home. The building has since been remodeled and is now the residence of the manager of Ole Bull State Park. A small tributary that runs behind the home and enters into Kettle Creek has been named Joerg Run.

OLSON FAMILY

When Martin and Hermania Brada Olson heard the news of Ole

Bull forming a colony in America, they sold their farm and house in Solor, Norway, and set sail on the *Incognito* to join the famed musician. Their youngest child, Burt, accompanied them; his brother and sister, Ole and Marie, were left behind with family members.

Martin Olson opened a blacksmith shop in Oleana, but found that he needed a second job to support his family. Months later, he was killed in a pine log slide accident at Layfield Hollow. As Bull's colony unraveled, Hermania Olson and son Burt moved to Germania, where she became a cook for Dr. Charles Meine during the organization of that village.

In 1856, Hermania Olson married Ezra H. Pritchard, one of the more interesting characters of the region. Pritchard is reputed to be the first person to take up residence in Stewardson Township. He had migrated from Connecticut and built a cabin on Jenkins Hill in Eulalia Township, south of Coudersport. A talented marksman and fisherman, Pritchard moved to the Kettle Creek valley because of the abundant wildlife. After the turnpike was built, he opened a blacksmith shop and wagon repair business along the road.

Hermania sent money back to Norway to pay for daughter Marie's trip to the U.S. Marie Olson went to work for Daniel F. Glassmire at the Coudersport Hotel and eventually married C. A. Burrous, first cousin of the famous naturalist, John Burroughs. Ole Olson arrived from Norway with his family sometime in the 1860s and settled in the Kettle Creek valley to start his own farm. He became a U.S citizen in 1879 and was hired as a newspaper editor in Tioga County, Pa., eventually relocating to Baltimore, Md., where he died in 1905.

Ole and Ella Olson had five children: Mary, Edward, Ezra, Etta and Henry. Their youngest, Henry, married Ida Bartholemew (widow of Theodore Wingert). For almost a quarter-century, Henry and Ida Olson operated "Olson Lodge," a bed and breakfast along the turnpike in Oleana.

Henry Olson was remembered fondly by Harry Kinney, another long-time Stewardson Township resident who died in 1991. In a 1987 interview, Kinney shared this anecdote:

Bull, the teenager, was more interested in music than in his studies.

This is Ole Bull's birthplace. His family's home was part of a prominent pharmacy operated by his father in downtown Bergen. The doorway (inset) depicts a swan that gave the building the name "Svanepotek"

Johan Storm Bull, Ole's father, was a respected apothecary in Bergen.

Ole Bull's mother, Anna.

By age 24, Bull was a willing subject for artists and photographers.

Many portraits of Ole Bull are on display in the U.S. and Norway.

Felicie was a mere 14 when she attracted Bull's attention.

Knud Bull was a talented landscape artist who ran afoul of the law.

Bull presented this portrait to Mrs. Edward Joerg. It now hangs in a Masonic hall at Coudersport, Pa.

Felicie Bull was often alone in tending to the children's needs. She's shown with (from left) Alexander, Eleonore Felicie, Lucie and Thorvald.

Ole Bull at about the time he married Felicie.

Thorvald Bull perished at sea.

Ole and Felicie Bull's daughters Eleonore Felicie Bull (above) and Lucie (below).

Ole Bull was a commanding figure.

This scene from the Coudersport and Jersey Shore Turnpike (now Pa. Route 44) shows the vast expanses of undeveloped forest land onto which the colonists descended.

At the height of his career, Ole Bull was known around the world.

The Oleana Hotel was the community's main gathering place.

Dr. Edward Joerg remained in the Oleana area after the other settlers had departed.

This house, identified in some accounts as Ole Bull's "castle," is probably in reality one of the homes that were occupied by New Norway settlers.

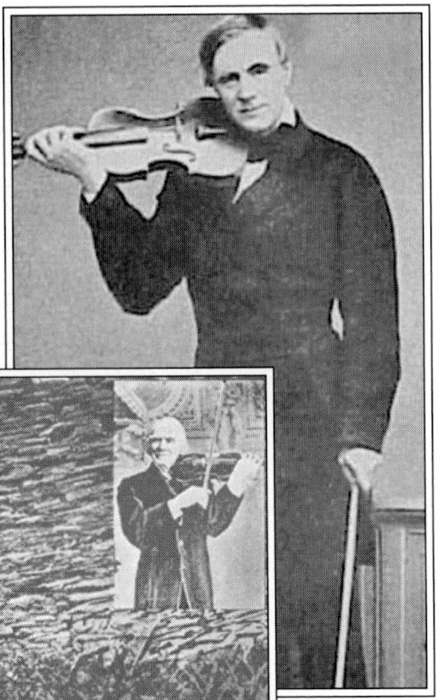

Ole Bull poses with his violin at the midpoint of his career.

The retaining wall built to support Ole Bull's hillside cabin is shown in this newspaper photo.

The "stone house" at Valhalla has been rebuilt after its destruction by fire and is the home of the Ole Bull State Park manager.

Blair Wisc. ? where located

This log cabin in Blair, Wisc., was the home of Sever Everson and his wife, the former Helen Petersdatter Anderson (at right). They met aboard the *Incognito* and were married at Ole Bull's colony. They relocated to Blair six years later. Many Norwegian immigrants stayed at the Everson home until they built houses of their own in the Blair area.

This is Mr. and Mrs. Ole Snyder and family. Snyder, son of Norwegian immigrants, was adopted by a Potter County family.

Bull went on tour with Maurice Strakosch and young Adelina Patti in 1852 to raise money for Oleana.

Pastor Jacob Aall Ottesen is shown seated at far left during a gathering of ministerial families at Madison, Wisc., in 1874.

Here is Ole Bull just before he left Norway for the U.S. to begin work on his New Norway/Oleana colony.

ABOVE: Most of the homes that were built by the New Norway settlers were not as large as this one, occupied by the Ole Olson family. The photo was found in the files of the Potter County Historical Society.

RIGHT: Hans Hansen Jr. (seated, right), son of a colonial family from Denmark, was a Union soldier in the Civil War. He settled in Roulette Township, Pa., in an area now known as Hansen Hollow. This photo was supplied by Ernest O. Mosch, grandson of Ruth Moran, Hansen's daughter (white dress).

A proud man who did not shy away from the camera, Ole Bull stood tall and erect.

This is the last cabin standing from the Oleana colony, located at New Bergen (Cartee Camp). Just weeks after this structure was photographed by William D. Fish of Coudersport, it was destroyed by fire.

Bull, center, appeared with the Trondheim (Norway) Symphony Orchestra, posing here with Peter Bjornson and accompanist/composer Martin A. Udbye (right).

The German Bible that was once Ole Bull's was donated to the Potter County Historical Society.

Ole Bull's son Alexander became an outstanding violinist in his own right.

Ole Bull

Bull's second wife, Sara

Ole, Sara and some gentlemen at Madison, Wisc.

Ole Bull gives a lesson to the daughter of New York Philharmonic conductor Robert Doremus.

Little has changed over the years at the concert hall of the Bull home (Valestrand) on Osteroy Island. It's now the private residence of Ole Bull's great-great-grandson, Knut Hendriksen.

Ole Bull (right, black hat) was a gracious host at the family's Valestrand home, which is still standing today.

Family members gather at the home of Ole and Sara Bull on Lysoen Island in 1875. Note the Norwegian flag with the United States flag embedded in its corner.

Ole Bull (1810-1880), in a portrait taken near the end of his remarkable career.

Elaborate carved wood and other adornments make the Bull home on Lysoen Island one of a kind. The residence is now a museum.

Even in his later years, Bull demonstrated advanced skills as a violinist and appealed to a variety of social classes.

This photograph was taken just months before Ole Bull's death at the age of 70.

The operators of the Edvard Grieg Museum in Norway pay tribute to Ole Bull with a photo display (below) and narrative detailing Bull's influence on the great musician. A statue of Grieg greets visitors to his former home.

(ABOVE) The name lives on today in a popular folk song as well as the Oleana Sweater Company, with many retail outlets, including this one in Bergen, Norway.

(LEFT) Evergreen boughs are always seen at the gravesite of Ole Bull (1810-1880) in Bergen.

Bergen, located along the North Sea in western Norway, is the nation's second largest city.

Ole Bull's widow, Sara, and his son, Alexander, performed during a dedication ceremony for this statue at Loring Park in Minneapolis.

Ole Bull's statue in downtown Bergen casts a shadow over a plaza and street also named in his honor.

This fish market along the harbor at Bergen continues a tradition that dates back more than three centuries.

Kelly (left) and Casey Kio, descendants of Norwegian immigrants, who grew up just miles from the Oleana colony, visited the Lysoen Museum. They're flanking the statue of Sylvea Bull Curtis, who donated the island and Bull's home to the Norwegian Society for the Protection of Ancient Monuments.

The beautiful wood grain of this piece at Ole Bull's home on Lysoen Island is a sight to behold.

Thousands of people paid tribute to Ole Bull and his colonists during a well-publicized "pilgrimage" in 1920. The scene was captured by photographer William D. Fish.

Researcher, historian, writer and lecturer Paul Engelstad visits the Olson family plot at the Oleana Cemetery.

The stone foundation is all that remains at the site of Ole Bull's "castle" on Nordjenskald Mountain in Potter County, Pa.

For many years, the American and Norwegian flags flew side by side at the site of Ole Bull's home in Potter County, Pa.

Ole Bull was content to spend his later years as a performer, social commentator and family man.

This photo was taken during author Paul W. Heimel's 2002 trip to Bergen, Norway. At left is Berit Hogheim, curator of the Lysoen Museum, established in Ole Bull's home on an island off the coast of Norway. At right is Olea Smith-Kaland, great-granddaughter of Ole Bull and his widow Sara.

Henry was a very caring man. There was a time when I was down and out after a fire had destroyed my store, bar and everything else I owned. I just about let it ruin me. I didn't much care if I lived or died. One day, Henry Olson came to me and said, "Harry, you are a bum. Are you going to let this kill you? If you will quit drowning your sorrows in the booze, I will help you out." The next day, he loaned me the money to buy a load of lumber and we started rebuilding the store. If it wouldn't have been for Henry Olson, I don't think I would have made it.

Olson had a deep interest in the activities of his ancestors. In 1934, he wrote to a friend that he had spent many years "trying to prove that Ole Bull knew what he was doing when he figured those Norwegians wanted a hilly country to live in— I'm staying!"

After he died in 1938, his widow continued to operate Olson Lodge, assisted by her granddaughter, Alice (Wingert) Hayes.

The youngest of Martin and Hermania Olson's children, Burt Olson, also remained in the area. On October 4, 1868, he married Catharine Steele. Burt Olson dealt in timber for a number of years and served one term on the Potter County Board of Commissioners (1882-85).

After his appointment as postmaster at the Kettle Creek Post Office in 1890, Olson was successful in changing its name back to the Oleana Post Office. Burt Olson also served as editor and publisher of a newspaper, the *McKean County Miner*, until about 1900. He died two years later in Chattanooga, Tenn. A newspaper obituary described him as "a bighearted gentleman missed by his friends."

OLE LYNN SNYDER

Jens Lamoe, a friend of Ole Bull in Norway, arrived at Oleana in 1852. Lamoe was joined by his wife Serene, who was several months pregnant, along with their two sons. When the Lamoes applied for citizenship papers in Coudersport, they changed their last names to Moe.

Theirs was apparently the first baby born in Ole Bull's colony, in October 1852. A fair-haired boy with Norwegian features, he was named

Ole Lind Moe, in honor of his godparents, Ole Bull and Swedish singing sensation Jenny Lind. When Serene Moe died, the young boy was adopted by a farm couple, Mr. and Mrs. Michael Snyder of Sweden Township, and renamed Ole Lynn Snyder.

Ole attended local schools in Potter County, where he demonstrated superior academic ability. He was a member of the first class to graduate from Lock Haven Normal School and went on to study law at the University of Michigan. Upon his return to northcentral Pennsylvania, he opened a law office in McKean County, just west of Potter County, and became a prominent citizen in the community of Port Allegany. He served as burgess, postmaster and a town councilman.

In 1884, Snyder joined the law firm of H.C. Dornan and M.J. Colcord, working out of a branch office in Coudersport. Three years later, he relocated to Buffalo to join another firm, S.W. Smith and John Ormerod, the latter of whom would become Judge of Potter County. Snyder became a law partner of the firm Stoddard, Snyder and Kinsey in Buffalo and branched out into other business and politics. Ole Snyder returned to Port Allegany late in life and enjoyed a pleasant retirement.

Snyder developed a deep interest in his Norwegian roots and conducted research into the Ole Bull colony. One of his prized possessions later in life was a violin that was said to belong to Ole Bull.

In 1910, he attempted to contact his brother, Peter J. Moe, in Springfield, Minn., but his letter went unanswered. Snyder later discovered an obituary showing that his brother had died on Jan. 27, 1910.

Snyder dug deeper. He discovered that both his father and his brother Peter had moved from Oleana to Stoughton, Wisc., while Seward Moe, his other brother, stayed behind in Oleana with another family.

His biological father, Jens Moe, joined Company K of the Third Regiment of Wisconsin during the Civil War. He was seriously wounded in battle and died in 1868. Peter Moe moved to Brown County, Minn., serving as a town clerk for 18 years, county commissioner and justice of the peace in Burnstown, prior to moving to Springfield.

Mrs. Norman Moe, who authored family archives donated to the

Potter County Historical Society, reported that the two boys were sometimes locked inside the family's cabin at Oleana while their father went off to work in the woods.

STEPHENSON FAMILY

Ole Stephenson (Steffensen) and his seven-year-old son William O. Stephenson came from Norway on the *Incognito*, tried to operate a farm at Oleana, and joined four or five other families for the trip to the Midwest in late 1853. The Stephensons took up residence in Madison, Wisc.

At the age of 16, William Stephenson enlisted in the 23rd Wisconsin Regiment, serving through the campaigns of Vicksburg and Mobile and more than a dozen smaller engagements before being discharged because of his youth. He promptly re-enlisted, giving his age as 18, and served until the end of the war.

"Slavery, the burning question before the country, did not sit well with the Norwegian settlers," William Stephenson told a newspaper reporter. "They were unanimously opposed to it, having many of them migrated to America to escape the hardships of strict government in their homeland."

"I was just a little shaver," he said of his Oleana experiences. "It seems that a leading citizen of our province and famous violinist, Ole Bull, had purchased a large tract of land, some 11,000 acres, from American agents, and was organizing a band of emigrants to settle it. My father, along with about 300 others, joined and the trip across the Atlantic was made. All personal property, furniture and what machinery they could carry was taken along . . . Farms were laid out and we began our homes. The farms soon showed signs of improvement when a great difficulty developed. Ole Bull in buying the land had gotten it from land sharks. When it came to proving up on our farms, it could not be done. The whole deal was a dead duck as far as getting our rights went."

Stephenson said the settlers heard reports of plentiful land and prosperous cities in the Lake Region of Wisconsin. "It was the period of western migration and some remarkable descriptions of the country hereabouts (Madison) were given to us out there. The Ole Bull settlement was completely abandoned and all came out this way . . . As to the Ole Bull settlement, I should say it was the victim of much crookedness then common. It is hard to say just what future it might have had were it not for the land title being defective."

IRGENS FAMILY

Ole Irgens, a grandson of the prominent pastor of the same name, was a schoolteacher in Modum, Norway, who moved with his wife and 17-year-old son Johan S. Irgens to Chicago, Ill., in 1849. The Irgenses ended up in Oleana for a short time and relocated to Austin in Mower County, Minn., where Ole died in 1871 at the age of 72. His wife, the former Henriette Calmeyer, died in 1875.

Johan S. Irgens became second lieutenant for the Union Army in the Civil War, but was discharged in 1862 due to a hearing impairment. Irgens went on to serve in the Minnesota State Legislature and was later named Secretary of State for Minnesota.

HANSEN FAMILY

The Hans Hansen family (sometimes spelled "Hanson") were among Danish passengers on the *Incognito* who settled in Oleana. There were two sons, Ole Hansen and Hans Hansen Jr. The elder Hans was connected to the Baptists in Denmark and in Wisconsin. The family lived in Store Verlose, Holbaekamt, Sjaelland, two Danish miles from Ringstad. Both Hans Hansen Jr. and Ole Hansen officially became U.S. citizens in 1858.

On Feb. 12, 1858, in Abbott Township, Ole Hansen married Olea (Olia) Iversdotter Johnson. She had come to the U.S. on the *Incognito* with her husband, John Carlsson, who died, leaving Olea to raise two daughters. She was 12 years older than Ole Hansen.

A daughter, Anna Christiana Hansen, was born on Christmas Day 1858. She married John Calvin Burt and relocated to Roulette Township, on the west side of Potter County, near the Allegheny River. Ole

Hansen bought a general store there and John Calvin Burt eventually purchased the business. Hans Hansen Jr. also relocated from Oleana to Roulette Township, and continued farming there in the community of Burtville late into his life.

Both of the Hansen sons enlisted in the Union Army. Hans Hansen Jr. registered as a private with Company K, 58th Regiment, Volunteers of Pennsylvania, in November 1861. He was promoted to corporal in March 1862 , sergeant that November and captain in January 1866. Hans Hansen Jr. became a member of the United Brethren in Christ.

Ole Hansen joined his brother's Company K, Volunteers of Pennsylvania, on Sept. 10, 1864. He signed off in Manchester, Va., on July 12, 1865. Torstein Jahr, in researching the Ole Bull colony for the magazine *Symra*, interviewed Hans Hansen Jr. at Burtville.

"I was too young to remember much then," Hansen said. "My take on Ole Bull? He was too kind; he did too much for the colonists." Asked about Bull's concerts to aid the colonists and rumors that the money and goods did not all arrive at Oleana, Hansen replied: "I do not know. I heard he had those concerts. If help did not arrive, you had to trust yourself and work hard. They were sponging on Ole Bull, too many of them. Father was working that winter by Renovo, 40 miles from Oleana, on the railroad. We lived on potatoes and salt most of the winter. Once, he came home with a 50-pound big bag of flour. It was like a big party."

Hans Hansen Sr. died in May 1889. Given his background, he may have been responsible for the formation of the first Danish Baptist church congregation in America in Oleana not long after most of the colonists had departed. In *Danish Baptists History in America*, a book by Nels Saerensen Lawdahl (Morgan Park, Ill., 1909), the author wrote:

The first glimpse of Baptists came to us through the woods of Pennsylvania. This is the state where the first Danish Baptists congregation got established. We will let Father Br. H. P. Andersen tell:

"As far as we know, in Abbott Township, Potter County, Pa., in the famous colony of Ole Bull (is) the first Danish Baptist congregation in

America. Nine Danish Baptists settled here in 1854. They all came from Sjaelland. Their names are: Christian Jensen and wife, Nels Nielsen and wife from Skee Old, Ned Peterson and wife. He was a blacksmith in Udstrup before he left. Jens Petersen from Lerhuset in Udstrup and Peter Johansen and wife. He is still living, but the wife is dead. These siblings organized a regular Baptist congregation after their arrival. An American Baptist priest, C. S. Thomas, and C. H. Reer, who was sent by the American Baptist publishers in Philadelphia, were present and helped with the organization. Brother Rayer was elected the congregation's leader. And the fruits of their work were soon visible. Nels Hansen, who later joined the Adventists, was baptized together with Caroline Johansen.

"But it could not have been God's intention to have a congregation among the people in the woods of Pennsylvania. One after the other of the members went west for more bread and an easier life. Christian Jensen and wife and Peter Johansen and wife went to Saxeville, Wisconsin, and after three years, all were spread around. We don't know how many of the brothers and sisters are still alive, but just let us say, 'Bless their memory!' They did not doubt God's son and his preaching, which consists of the following, 'they did what they could do'."

The 'Brother Rayer' mentioned by Andersen is actually Charles Henry Reer, a Dane who was an agent for the American Tract Society. He married Mary Peterson in Cartee Camp in 1856 and signed on in Company F, 9th Regiment in January 1856. His citizenship papers were issued in 1860. Reer signed off from Company F in September 1865. He died in January 1897. The couple's son, Walter Reer, became a Baptist priest.

JENS JACOBSEN SKOIEN

Skoien and his family remained at Oleana until 1854, owning 50 acres, one of which was plowed, and a cow. He apparently never built his house; his family spent the 1853-54 winter with friends at New Bergen. The Skoiens traveled west with C. F. Solberg in 1854, joining their Norwegians counterparts in Rock Prairie, Wisc. They later relocated with a number of other families to Freeborn County, Minn., and operated a large farm there.

Jens enlisted in Company K of the 15th Wisconsin during the Civil War in 1861. He participated in numerous battles in Tennessee and Kentucky before being taken prisoner during the Battle of Chickamauga (Ga.) on Sept. 20, 1863. While he was held at a Richmond, Va., prison camp, Skoien contracted typhoid fever. He was admitted to a prison hospital in Danville, Va., where he died on Feb. 16, 1864.

His wife, Gina, died in 1871. Her sister Sofie married an American; she died in 1871.

OTHER SETTLERS

Elizabeth Baker Case was among the last survivors of the Ole Bull colony. Arriving in the settlement as a child, she was left with a German family in Germania upon the demise of Bull's settlement while her parents moved on. They intended to find a home and then return to claim her. Elizabeth waited for several years, but she never saw her parents again. She ended up moving to Coudersport and marrying W.A. Case.

Among others who stayed according to the records of the Potter County Historical Society, were H. Larsen, the gardener, and the family of N. B. Suhr, who had a farm at New Bergen (Carter Camp).

Gradually, those who remained became sewn into the cultural and social fabric of the region. Nellie Burt Maltby (daughter of John Calvin Burt), in her newspaper interview at Jersey Shore, lamented that some of the children and grandchildren of the pioneers went on to attend schools with the Germans in Germania. They learned to speak German and, in some cases, lost their Norwegian or Danish names. In many instances, she wrote, the younger Scandinavians never knew their great-grandparents' names.

Ole Olsen Teppen as well as Syver and Iver Iversen (from Vaaler) stuck it out in Oleana until 1858, while Tosten Torrison Forkerud and Helge Opland stayed until 1859. Those five ended up in the Blair/Coon

Valley region of Wisconsin, the biggest Solung settlement in the U.S. Their priest, the Rev. Erik Jensen, wrote, "Ole Bull's love had helped them over to the colony in Oleana, Pa., and they shared with him the loss of losing something they had worked for in many years."

Another priest, the Rev. Adolph Bredesen, reported to Torstein Jahr that two members of his congregation, Iver Olsen Holte and his brother Knud Olsen, had moved from Oleana to the Wisconsin communities of Arkdale (Colombia County) and Stoughton. Rev. Bredesen was two years old when he traveled with his parents on the *Incognito* in 1852. The Bredesens rejected the enticements of Ole Bull and John Holfeldt and instead moved on from New York City to the Solung settlement in Roche a Cree, Wisc.

Helene Anderson Petersdatter from Valer/Svenbykarne, who came on the *Incognito* with her family, met her future husband, Syver Everson, on the ship. The two were wed at Oleana and remained at the colony until 1858, when they relocated to Blair, Wisc. Once they were settled there, their small log home became a way station for other Norwegians. School classes and church services were occasionally held there.

Colonists Mr. and Mrs. Arne Kjelson, Iver Everson, Ole Olsen Teppen, Ole Peterson, Ebrat Peterson and Anders Olsen also resettled in the Blair area. A year later, colonists Tosten Torrison Forkerud and Helge Opland joined them. Everhardt P. Lieberg from Solor was 19 when he arrived in Oleana. He volunteered for service in the Civil War, advancing to the rank of captain. Lieberg was injured in Altoona, Pa. He died in Mankato, Minn., in 1906.

Halfdan Alfred Eckholdt was nine years old when he came to Oleana with his parents. They moved on to Minnesota where, after his father's death, Halfdan joined his mother in operating a store until enlisting in the Minnesota Volunteers during the Civil War. After three years of service, he enrolled at the University of Michigan, earned his law degree, and went on to enjoy a long career in Olmstead County and Rochester, Minn. Eckholdt was active in Republican politics, the Baptist Church and the Masonic Fraternity/Knights Templar. He also served for a time as County Attorney in Olmstead County. He and his wife, the former Adeline Lane, had seven children. Among them were: Walter, who served as Olmstead County Register of Deeds; F.R., an attorney who practiced in Florida; Ella, who married Harry Dinsdale, a civil engineer; Irving L., a lawyer who practiced in Rochester; Laura, a public schoolteacher.

Colonist Hr. N. Nielsen, identified in some accounts as a friend of Ole Bull's, ended up in Buffalo, N.Y.

Ole Snyder wrote of E. P. Sebery, who became captain of Company C, Third Minnesota Volunteers.

There are scant records of other colonists. In June 1858, the following colonists became U.S. citizens in Potter County: Iver Olsen, Helge Knudsen, Daniel Ericksen, Carl Carlsen, Halvor Mattesen, Knud Helgesen and Swedes Andres Olsen and Peter Peterse. On Sept. 23, 1859, Norwegian colonists Ole Helgesen and Helge Elesen received their citizenship papers; Danes John Carl Anton Kreidel and Nels Peterson in 1860; Frantz Mathias Jansen from Schleswig, Germany, in 1861; Dane Simon Petersen and Norwegians John Iversen and John G. Cosolowsky in 1863; Dane Niels Christian in July 1864; Norwegian Nelson Larsen in 1865; Dane Christian Broderson in 1866.

Colonist Peter Anderson died at the colony and is buried in the small cemetery at Oleana.

And, finally, August Svendsen, believed to be the last of the Oleana colonists, lived by himself in the forest for many years. An article on page one of the Jan. 8, 1904 edition of the *Port Allegany Argus*, reported the death by freezing of "August Swanson, an aged hermit. Reportedly the last survivor of Ole Bull's colony. Swanson became a hermit after the colony failed and the castle was abandoned. He was seen only once in 17 years prior to his death." Two timber workers found his body. Another newspaper article attributed his death to starvation.

Twelve

One of the most persistent and distorted stories of the Ole Bull colony surrounds the hillside home which Bull is said to have occupied— often referred to as "Ole Bull's Castle." Newspaper articles, correspondence and other documentation paint a fairly clear picture of this structure, which hardly resembled a castle in a traditional sense. The home was not intended as a permanent residence for Bull, but rather as a place where he could rest when he was not engaged in a concert tour or otherwise occupied.

A two-story log cabin did serve as a temporary home for Bull, part of a vague plan to erect a larger structure that would eventually include a massive music hall on the shelf of Nordjenskald Mountain. The building measured 36 feet by 20 feet and was constructed mostly of rough, hand-hewn white pine. The roof was of a four-square design and spacious porches surrounded the building. A deep water well was dug nearby and a small barn erected. A road leading up the mountain skirted a small creek known today as Ole Bull Run.

A perpendicular cliff on which the cabin was built had to be bolstered with thousands of unmortared stones, testimony to the patience and hard work of some of the colonists. The wall alone was an impressive sight from the valley below and its presence could account for the frequent references to the home as a castle.

The crest of this bluff afforded a commanding view of the valley for miles around. Behind the structure were two tall mountains. Nearby was Lyso Spring, a small natural water source named by Bull after the Island of Lysoen, where he would draw his last breath.

A quarter-century after the cabin was built, publisher and historian W. W. Thompson was among a delegation of Potter County citizens who traveled across Kettle Creek and up the mountainside to see what remained of Ole Bull's home. His August 1877 account follows:

The castle of Ole Bull, the world renowned violinist, was finally reached and after gathering a few pounds of old nails, pieces of old shingles, a bushel or two of ferns for souvenirs, there was time to examine the place. All that now remains of the building is very little to go crazy over. There is a cellar perhaps 20 feet by 30 feet in size, partially filled with ferns, underbrush and weeds in profusion. The cellar wall still remains in good condition; some of the sills are yet in place; and scattered about may be seen pieces of lumber, old shingles and general rubbish which once constituted the building. In digging the cellar, quartz rock was found containing a little gold—so at least reported—but for some reason the matter was never thoroughly investigated.

The original clearing was but little larger than required for a house. A few yards east is a high bluff descending almost perpendicular about 100 feet to the stream. Along the brink of bluff a stone wall was built about 40 yards in length, in some places 15 to 20 in height on the lower side, and a foot or two above the surface on the upper side. Originally there were steps down to the water but there are no signs of any now.

From the building the ground sloped in any direction though but little back. A few yards back is a bench of comparatively level land, consisting of 50 to 75 acres. If Ole Bull had remained, this probably would have been a fine farm. Across from a slight depression was the well, now filled in, and the farm of which nothing remains.

To reach the place a winding road was built from the stream some distance above, of easy grade, and near the castle wide enough for three teams abreast. It is about 24 years since this work was done and the road has grown up to brush and is blocked by fallen trees. Near the house where the road was may now be found trees three to five inches in diameter.

In the Aug. 11, 1920, edition of the *Potter County Journal*, Samuel Haven Glassmire, whose novel "Olea" was based in part on actual developments at Oleana, continued his crusade against the harsh findings of Dr. George Donehoo, founder of the Potter County Historical Society. Glassmire looked into the history of Bull's mountainside cabin and reported the following:

Dr. Donehoo is mistaken when he states that the famous castle was not completed. It was not only substantially completed and ornamented, but was partially furnished. I have it from eyewitnesses that Ole Bull himself stayed there and played there on several occasions. It is true that he did not actually reside there as he had intended, for his concert tours in the interest of his colony called him away. This is the answer to the constant question, "Where is Ole Bull?"

And the castle itself was not a crude, unfinished log cabin. It was a pretentious two-story frame structure with wide porches and a basement hewed out of solid rock. It was papered and decorated inside with a heavy material of a curious Norse design, relics of which I have seen. The immense castle wall around the crest of the mountain and the well-built road winding up to it, which exist today, mutely testify to Norwegian workmanship and skill, and to the anxious plans of the great musician.

In 1941, an article originally appearing in the *Altoona Mirror* on May 30 was reprinted in the June 21 edition of the *Potter County Journal*. Henry W. Shoemaker, the nation's first state folklorist, had apparently visited the site and inquired about the home's particulars during discussions with area residents. Excerpts of his flowery article follow:

Oleana

The dimensions of Ole Bull's castle can be measured by the foundations, although only the central wing was completed. The construction was of cut mountain stone, a story and a half high, with tower of wood, the sides converging to a point. From the apex of the tower issued the top of a 70-foot stick of white pine, its butt imbedded in the cellar floor, and 30 feet above the tower's culminating point, from whence daily floated the glorious stars and stripes. No Norwegian flags were in evidence. Old Glory was furled at sunset through a hinged trap-door in the sloping roof.

Huge double doors, glass-lighted and French windows were almost the height of the ground floor, with circular windows in the low-ceilinged sleeping rooms above. The central high-ceilinged room was used as a music room. At the ends of each wing were to have been vast open fireplaces 12 feet by 12 feet. One wing was to be a musical library, the other a gun and trophy room. The three wings were to open into one another, and the stove and fireplaces furnish heat for all.

The upper rooms were to be heated by small stoves, or from registers in the floors. The finish was white pine, stained natural color, like Ole Bull's studio in Bergen, Norway. This writer has seen a few pieces of the woodwork, saved from the fire of 1903, which destroyed the interior of the state forest ranger's house at Walhalla, constructed from the stones and woodwork of the dismantled castle . . .

A perfect picture on reduced scale of the one completed wing of Ole Bull's castle exists— the barn of Henry Andresen, the maestro's secretary, on the Germania Branch of Kettle Creek, several miles northeast of the ill-fated castle where Sonojoh (the Indian name) is crossed by the Jersey Shore-Coudersport Turnpike. Andresen sought to perpetuate the plan of the castle when he built his barn about 10 years after Ole Bull left. Ole Bull's steward, Olesen, laid out a graveyard that was filled after the first arduous winter when pneumonia and influenza ravaged the colony.

One legend tells of a beautiful troll, like a vampire or ghost, who induced a lad about to leave for the Ole Bull colony to marry her. She knew in her heart a troll could not cross water, but such was her love for this mortal that she was determined to go anyway. On the long sea voyage she commenced to age rapidly and was an old woman when the ship touched New York. As she grew old, her husband quickly became cool to her and flirted outrageously with all the flaxed-haired damsels on the ship. The long trip by train, canal and wagon to Oleana about used up her reserve strength and she was said to be the first of the colony to die at the new home. The gravediggers, well aware that she was a troll, buried her on the far side of the creek from the graveyard so that she would not come across the water and annoy her husband who soon after married a beautiful young girl.

In front of the castle was a flagstone terrace, with stone coupling, overlooking the valley of Kettle Creek; here Ole Bull often played the violin on moonlit nights. The original pines and hemlocks, obstructing the view of the valley and his favorite Lyso (water of light) spring below were slashed, but the remaining timber surrounding the castle was not removed until about 1900.

For the above information, the writer is indebted principally to Samuel H. Pfoutz of Kettle Creek, whose father cut logs for Ole Bull; to the late John H. Myers of Clinton County, who helped his father haul window sashes, staircases, tools and nails while the castle was being built; and to an old gentleman who resided on the Nichols place on Pine Creek, near Avis, also in Clinton County, who helped his father at the castle.

Eventually, the path leading to the cabin site was cleared and a marker was erected to briefly describe Ole Bull's experiences in Potter County. Later, that was replaced by a new marker that remains at the site today. For a time, the Norwegian and American flags flew from flagpoles erected near the cabin site. In the late 20th century, a Pennsylvania Conservation Corps crew made improvements to the path, installing drains, stabilizing the surface with crushed rock and building a bench to provide a resting area for tourists making the trek up the mountain.

All that remains at the site today are the crumbling, moss covered stone walls that formed a portion of the building's foundation. Periodically over the past half-century, efforts to persuade government or historical agencies to finance construction of a castle replica at the site have failed.

Thirteen

What became of the central figure in this story— the man whose dreams were the foundation of the Pennsylvania colonial experience?

Ole Bull, much to his dismay, found that he had lost some of his popularity and prestige not only in Norway, but also in many parts of the eastern United States. Bull was sad, disillusioned and humbled by the experience. However, contrary to much that has been written, the Oleana escapade did not leave him penniless. During two decades of performing, he had collected jewelry and many other material possessions of considerable value. In addition, he had haphazardly gathered thousand-dollar bonds and letters. Much of the fortune was kept in safekeeping by Bull's American friends while he was hounded by creditors, some from his Oleana settlement, who were intent on seizing whatever they could of his belongings.

Back in Norway, Felicie had sold the Andoen island home in order to support her and the children after they moved to Christiania.

Seeking receptive audiences and new adventures, Bull and Maurice Strakosch set out in early 1854 for the fast-developing western U.S. cities. They played for several sold-out houses in Chicago, the final concert there including a dinner in Bull's honor attended by 400 Americans and Norwegians. A performance in St. Louis was next, followed by a perilous trip to Panama, where Bull fell ill with yellow fever. He finally boarded a steamer bound for California in July for a two-month concert series, based in San Francisco. That city was an odd mix of wealthy families still riding the wave of newfound prosperity in the 1849 Gold Rush and transplanted easterners who yearned for the cultural enrichment they had enjoyed before relocating.

Another risky scheme, perhaps as unrealistic as Oleana, attracted Bull's attention in February 1855. Strakosch and another prominent musician, Max Maretsek, persuaded Ole to join them in founding an Italian Opera in New York. Bull became the main financier, leasing the Academy of Music. Still recovering from his illness and only vaguely familiar with opera, Bull left the management in others' hands. A performance of Verdi's "Rigoletto" opened to a small audience and, after a few weeks, the opera was closed. Putting the opera fiasco behind him, Bull scheduled a concert tour through midwestern U.S. cities, only to cancel the shows as he battled malaria. "I don't see any person except my servant, my door being always locked," he wrote to friend Anne Lynch Botta. "I am half dreaming but never sleeping, and the least rush makes me shudder. At last I shall be a coward or a madman. Past falls heavily upon me and I gaze with frantic enthusiasm in the future. My troublesome life and unsteady habits have long since taken hold of my body and soul and made me unfit for society, and still sometimes I feel very alone."

Still weak and depressed, Bull ended up back in Cambridge, Mass., visiting with the Longfellows in December 1855. Henry Wadsworth Longfellow, William Makepeace Thackery and prominent publisher James T. Fields were able to convince Ole that he should not deprive the world of his musical gifts. His savings depleted, Bull decided to set out on another concert tour through the U.S. As his health allowed, Bull and his company kept up a busy performance schedule. He catered to American audiences with a "Fantasia on American Airs," including segments of standards such as "Arkansas Traveler," "Pop Goes the Weasel" and "Home, Sweet Home."

Some critics said that mournfulness in his violin playing reflected his problems. "It is the peculiarity of Ole Bull and perhaps the secret of his charm over the sympathies of his audiences, that all he plays seems so faithfully autobiographic," wrote the *New York Evening Post.*

Ole had maintained little contact with his wife since he sailed from Norway, even though she sent letters reminding him of his obligations. "It seems to me that it must trouble you not to see your children for the years since you left and that it would be good if you could come back to see them," she wrote. In late 1856, their eldest son, Alexander, 17 years old, arrived at New York to help his father cope with his depression.

Clearly, Ole Bull was not well, as can be seen by this brief note an unidentified woman sent to a New York newspaper, published on Jan. 27, 1857:

Coming up Broadway a few days ago, I met Ole Bull, looking so pale that I scarcely knew him. He has been lying ill for three months at a little town on the Illinois River, and had recently arrived here, where his first greeting was to be arrested at the suit of a very doubtful claimant. He and his son, a very fine boy, dined with us the next day after I met him and we heard more of his recent history. Poor fellow! He says he has lost, in our "free country," all that he valued, his health, his money and his great name, and he is content now to seek refuge again at home in Norway.

One of Bull's few references to the Oleana colony following its failure appeared in a card he mailed to the *New York Times*, published in the April 15, 1857, edition, reading: "I have noticed, in several of the public papers, a statement to the effect that I have lost nothing by purchases of land in this country, but have actually sent large sums to Norway for investment. I know not who is the author of this report, but I think it due to the public and to myself to pronounce it wholly unfounded."

Two weeks later, in a letter to Riggs and Company, Bull spoke of a "relapse of fever" rendering him barely able to meet his concert obligations. He also referred to lingering debts to Maurice Strakosch and John Hopper. This letter revealed that a bust of George Washington seized from Bull for non-payment of debt had been returned to him. The bust was then delivered to his attorney and good friend E. W. Stoughton, who was described by Bull as "actively engaged in getting me out of the clutches of the law."

That Ole Bull was vulnerable to schemers was further demonstrated when he was persuaded that a large rock standing in the Taunton River, north the town of Fall River, Mass., was the first landing place for the Vikings in their discovery of America. Bull agreed to pay $50 for the rock, with the intention of having it shipped to the Royal Society in Denmark for public exhibition, but the rock remains in its place.

On July 29, 1857, Ole Bull and his son Alexander boarded the steamer *America* in Boston for a return trip to Norway. Bull, his hair now mostly gray, did not know what to expect after a seven-year absence punctuated by the Oleana experience. To the conservative establishment, which was facing a growing revolt from rural rebels and young intellectuals, the failure of Bull's colony was welcome news. They regarded him as their challengers' hero and resented not only his efforts to establish Oleana, but also Bull's Norwegian theater and the larger issue of emigration. Therefore, the conservatives reveled in his failures and spread the notion that he had speculated ruthlessly at the expense of his countrymen.

Arriving in Christiania, Bull deposited his son with the rest of the family and left to resume his direction of the Bergen Theater. Soon afterwards, an article appeared in the Christiania newspaper, *Morgenbladet*. It read:

No one has welcomed Bull. Is this to be the first time? There was a time when the papers had no more previous news than about Ole Bull (even as) he had flown out to be our land's springtime messenger in melody. Even if Bull is in the position of wishing to forget, we are in the position of wishing to remember what he has done for his country and for every single individual . . . If, like the butterfly who in magic remembrance of the sunlight fluttered toward the candle, only to find that it burned, burned terribly, it is only the more reason for us to receive him with love. Home must be a consolation to one who has suffered, for he has exile in his soul. And if he is lovingly received by us, the painful memories will soon be dispelled in a new poem . . . for this is the poet's way of remembering when one allows him to be a poet.

Ole was impressed with the greeting and inquired about its author, Bjornstjerne Bjornson (1832-1910). He learned that Bjornson was a social commentator and author who had agitated against Danish performers in Norwegian theater. At the same time, Henrik Ibsen had left the Norwegian Theater at Bergen to pursue a similar opportunity in Christiania. Bull, still the formal owner of the Bergen facility, recruited Bjornson to take over as its director and instructor and finally returned to Christiania in February 1858.

The people of the nation's capital were lukewarm toward Bull, although an appearance at the Freemasons' Hall generated a great deal of enthusiasm, particularly when he performed Paganini's "E-flat Major Concerto." Bull was pleased to see that the new Christiania Norwegian Theater, under the direction of Henrik Ibsen, was a modest success.

Back in the public eye, Bull was once again subjected to the reviews of writers wherever he performed. One of his harshest critics was the noted German, Eduard Hanslick, who had heard Bull in 1840 and then observed an 1858 concert in Vienna:

Ole Bull was always given to one-sided virtuosity, to a combination of sovereign bravura and bizarre manners, which might be called "Paganinic." Enthusiasm for this kind of thing, which leaves the heart and mind untouched and excites only surprise, has decreased astonishingly during the last twenty years . . . We demand of a virtuoso, himself insignificant as a composer, that he place his technical abilities at the service of superior music. Now, as he did twenty years ago, Ole Bull plays only his own compositions. Bull's muse is consistent only in two things: inconsistency of musical construction and preponderance of bravura.

His concertos are similarly formless fantasies, indulging partly in broadly expansive adagios, partly in antiquated bravura . . . There are two techniques which he favors: harmonics and double-stops. Both are executed with brilliant security and purity . . . Still more brilliant are his staccatos, which he renders unsurpassably, both up-bow and down-bow. His tone has a beautiful softness. By way of summation we can say that his virtues are purely technical. The whole orientation of his playing has become obsolete, and it needs all his personal charm to recall it even partially to a fictitious life.

In June 1858, Bull visited his childhood friend, Consul Alexander Grieg, at Landas, outside of Bergen, primarily because Grieg's 15-year-old son Edvard had been publicized as a child prodigy. He was impressed with the young man's compositions and persuaded his parents to send Edvard to Leipzig to study music. By that time, Bull was more determined than ever that Norway should generate its own musical art and he was preparing the ground for the emergence of true Norwegian music.

Bull finally acquired the Valestrand estate from his mother in 1858. He and his family stayed there through the winter. In May 1859, Bjornson's classic peasant novel *Arne* appeared, dedicated to Bull in gratitude for the confidence he had shown in the author. Bjornson's interest in Norwegian politics drew him back to Christiania. With Bull, Ibsen and Bjornson out of the picture, the Norwegian Theater at Bergen (renamed the National Stage by that time) struggled before closing its doors in 1863.

Back on the concert stage as he observed his 50th birthday in 1860, Bull bravely and successfully moved into Sweden and Denmark. He was back in Norway to receive the Order of St. Olav for "meritorious artistic activity" at the same time Karl XV was crowned as King of Norway and Sweden. Concert appearances in Germany and England followed. By the end of July 1861, Ole was back at Valestrand with Felicie and children while working on new compositions.

In October, he returned to the stage, traveling to England while Felicie and the children relocated to Christiania. There was a growing perception by this time that Bull was losing his luster. Audiences expected strict adherence to classical standards and a level of technical excellence that Bull had previously reached. As Mortimer Smith wrote:

In the presence of so many rivals Bull must have been keenly aware of the deficiencies of his own playing from the point of view of the classical school. He had long since ceased to play Beethoven and now but rarely ventured Mozart in public, and as for the newer composers like Mendelssohn or Schumann, it is doubtful if at any time he tried to play their compositions. But it is obvious from the programs of this period that he tried to subdue his eccentricities and to stress his own compositions less. The best he could do, however, was to use as his principal concert pieces the Mozart adagio which all his life was his principal concession to serious music, and Paganini's fantasia on "Di tanti polpiti."

When he did play his own compositions, the London critics did not go beyond calling them "wonderfully original displays." The general tenor of criticism was typified by the Musical World, *which remarked that those who heard so much good music were not likely to go a second time to hear playing which, "sacrificing everything intellectual to the mere trickery of execution, can never be dignified by the name of art." This paper's criticism is none the less valid for the fact that people DID go a second time to hear Bull, even serious professionals who deployed his "trickery," for his amazing executive abilities and marvelous poetic tone were still in themselves a delight and wonder.*

But here again the essential tragedy of Bull as a musician is impressed upon us, thrown into bold relief as it is by the presence of so many other great and serious artists. Unsurpassed mechanically, and with a nature that was all fire and poetic feeling, it was unfortunate that Bull's temperament was such that it did not allow him to submit to that patient and arduous training of sheer hard work in youth which is necessary in the development of any great musician.

While Ole worked his way through England, Felicie's health was declining as her relationship with her husband was deteriorating. Her letter to him in December detailed her depression and physical ailments. Bull responded with characteristic self-pity in a letter written on Feb. 7, 1862:

Pierced by deep sorrow and unspeakable pain I write you these lines. My hope of being able to stay with our children and to bring them up under my loving supervision has given way to discouragement. Whatever I do or how makes no difference. My debt is forever growing and I am defrauded of my receipts . . . From America I get nothing and poor prospects. Too much compliance on my part and the need to help others, while I forgot my own wants for the sorrows of other people, has been much to blame. How can I extricate myself from this painful position I do not know, for there are many machinations against me.

At home in Norway I have been persecuted when I was in trouble, for it was only when I could give that I was well regarded. And have I not had all my thoughts fixed on the interests of my native land? Yes, altogether too much. I neglected myself, my family, my affairs and my interests in order to raise the sense of the nationally beautiful. Hate, envy, and slander sought to distort and cripple my every action no matter how unimportant.

You could not understand; your friends were not my friends, but neither were they yours, for they did the worst thing they could do—they aroused a misunderstanding that separated us. If only I could come instead of this letter, how gladly I would do so! God bless you and make you strong and healthy! Your devoted Ole.

Bull set off for Paris soon after mailing the letter; Felicie never saw it. She died on Feb. 16, 1862, at the age of 44.

"Thus ended a marriage that was never satisfactory to either party but one which caused much more active unhappiness to the wife than to the husband," Mortimer Smith wrote. "Felicie was not cut out to be the partner of a temperamental artist, for she was at heart a simple and unsophisticated woman who wanted nothing beyond the homely pleasures of her house and children and the love of her husband. Within her limitations she was a good wife— almost a heroic wife, in view of what she had to contend with. Her married life was a long unrelieved record of unhappiness; it was not only that she was forced to live much of the time in a country that was foreign and hateful to her— the real tragedy was that she remained to the end passionately in love with a man who had long since outgrown his love for her."

Tragedy struck again on Dec. 26 of that same year when their second oldest child, Thorvald Bull, fell from the mast of a ship in the Mediterranean Sea and drowned.

"I tried to quiet myself with the thought that I did everything in my power to prevent his going to sea," Bull wrote in a letter to his son Alexander in February 1863, "but he would make his own way for himself."

Perhaps as a remedy for his turmoil and depression, Bull immersed himself in his music and his causes. His newest dream was a Norwegian Academy of Music to be located at Christiania. An article which appeared in the journal *Illustreret Nyhedsblad*, written by editor Jonas Lie but signed by Bull, read:

The history of our country's attitude toward art is a disgrace to the nation and a crime against those men who have given their all to art, and are driven to sell our honor abroad. My calling in this world is Norwegian music. I am no painter, no sculptor, no writer. I am a musician, and as such the Norwegian people should trust me when I say that I hear a wonderfully deep and characteristic sound board vibrating in the breasts of my people. The desire of my life has been to give it strings, that it might find a voice, and its deep tones penetrate the temple as Norway's church music bears the words of the minister to the hearts of the congregation.

I have spent my life in striving to overcome the denationalized musical taste and, with the other Norse artists, trying to climb these gray cliffs of indifference. I have in vain offered my assistance in conducting orchestras, in composing for the stage, in trying to educate the people in regard to their own heritage of music. Now I want to propose to my colleagues, the Norwegian musicians, that we join hands for the purpose of scaling the rocks and reaching the top; that we found an academy for instruction in music. Perhaps we shall at last succeed in planting our flag at the top; perhaps we shall be able to reach down and assist those who are toiling upward!

Once again, Bull sought financial support from the Norwegian Parliament, and once again it was rejected. Bergen had proven to be a difficult setting in which to stimulate an appreciation of Norwegian music; Christiania was even worse. Bull repeatedly ran up against the "gray cliffs of indifference," only adding to his frustrations.

On the other hand, Bull derived considerable pleasure in drawing up plans for a new structure to replace the family home at Valestrand. He contracted with his brother, Georg Andreas Bull, an architect, to design the home, which would copy the old Nordic style, with its cornices and dragon heads. The main hall would be designated as a "music room," with proper acoustics, designed in the old Viking style.

Henry Wadsworth Longfellow's affinity for Ole Bull is confirmed by his basing one of his most prominent works, "Tales of a Wayside Inn" (1863), on Bull. The fictional work explores the tales of characters who gather at an old Massachusetts inn. Bull was referred to as follows:

Last the Musician, as he stood
Illuminated by that fire of wood,
Fair-haired, blue-eyed, his aspect blithe;
His figure tall and straight and lithe;
And every feature of his face
Revealing his Norwegian race,

A radiance, streaming from within,
Around his eyes and forehead beamed,
The Angel with the violin,
Painted by Raphael, he seemed.
He lived in that ideal world
Whose language is not speech, but song.

During the summer of 1864, Bull relaxed at Valestrand, where the young Edvard Grieg was a frequent visitor. This was an important summer in Grieg's musical development. From the conservatory at Leipzig, he and Bull played Mozart trios together and spoke frequently of folk music and nationalism. Bull also introduced Grieg to folk music on the Hardanger fiddle and improvisation that suggested a path of his own composing. Their discussions also centered on the work that would be necessary to make the music academy at Christiania a reality.

Ole Bull was off to Germany, Vienna, Prague and the Netherlands during the 1864-65 winter, and was rejuvenated by the warm reception he received, during both his concert appearances and his off-hours.

Back at Valestrand the following summer, he laid out a grand scheme to improve the grounds, with his son Alexander to do much of the work. Alexander Bull was becoming an accomplished violinist in his own right. His father wrote him several letters relating his many instruments and experiments. The letters also reveal that Ole kept abreast of worldwide political affairs, which was to some extent an outgrowth of his personal acquaintance with many of the leading men of many European nations and his sympathy with the thoughts and experiences of the people.

Ole enjoyed the comfort and support of family and friends in 1866, spending most of the year in Norway with his mother during her final days, brothers and Bjornson, who by that time was directing the struggling theater at Christiania. A successful and satisfying concert series in Moscow followed. Bull enjoyed the Russian hospitality through the winter, composing additional music and experimenting with alterations in his violin's construction, then departed for Poland in May 1867.

The newspaper *Kurjer Warszawski*, after three concerts in Warsaw, reported:

It is now some twenty-five years since he last came. The first time he was in his best youth. Now his hair is gray. Even if his playing does not have the same youthful fire, it now resounds with greater calm and seriousness after many working years. Today, as before, he stands as the first.

In Polacca Guerriera the first theme especially was interpreted with such strength of tone and such fire of execution that in spite of his gray hair Ole Bull seemed like a young man. After the Carnival of Venice there was endless applause. It is with sorrow that we say farewell to the great master.

Bull returned to Valestrand in late summer 1867, conferring again with Edvard Grieg, who by that time had been able to generate enough support to schedule an opening of the music academy at Christiania. But Bull had other ambitions on his mind. The Oleana experience now 15 years behind him, and the U.S. Civil War concluded, he was anxious to return to America.

Fourteen

Ole Bull and his son Alexander arrived in New York on Dec. 11, 1867. Heartened by the audience reaction at three New York concerts, Bull set out for the Norwegian immigrant settlements in Wisconsin. Concerned that the Oleana experience had forever marred his image, Bull was pleasantly surprised by the warm reception he received.

After concert appearances in the smaller villages of Janesville and Stoughton, he moved on to Madison, where 100 torchbearers were on hand to escort him to his hotel. This was not uncommon, according to Sara Bull: "In many towns they met him with torchlight processions and speeches of welcome, and he often left substantial proofs of his sympathy in gifts to their churches and libraries."

Bull planned an ambitious concert tour that started in Chicago and Washington before performances in New York's Steinway Hall during March 1868. There, he was haunted by the echoes of Oleana in the form of a broadsheet that featured an account of the 1852-53 colonization effort. However, most people seemed inclined to look beyond the past and treated Bull as the grand old man of the American concert stage.

Back in Norway, Ole Bull's new home at Valestrand—five years in the planning and construction—was ready for occupancy. Buoyed by his American earnings and anxious to relax in his new island home, Bull set sail for Bergen soon after his concerts. He remained in Norway long enough to present his second daughter, Lucie, for marriage to a lawyer,

Peter Jacob Homann.

He returned to the U.S. in late 1868, spending several weeks with friends such as actor Edwin Booth, writer Anne Lynch Botto and New York Philharmonic President Robert Ogden Doremus. Bull also began to experiment with a bizarre scheme to alter the construction of the piano so as to create sound tone qualities that might more closely match those of the violin. For this endeavor, he contracted with John Ericsson, a prominent Swedish-American inventor who had designed and built the battleship *Monitor*, made famous during the Civil War. Only two pianos of this type were made, one of which is preserved at Bull's later home on Lysoen.

The following summer, Bull served as concertmaster for the massive Boston Peace Jubilee, held to celebrate the end of the Civil War. He led a 200-member violin section in the 1,000-piece orchestra, supporting a 10,000-voice choir. Bull then relaxed on the Isle of Shoals, off Portsmouth in New Hampshire, where he became acquainted with poet John Greenleaf Whittier.

In February 1870, Ole and Alexander Bull rode the newly opened Pacific Railroad to the growing city of San Francisco, Calif. Reviews of his performances there were invariably positive, including this item from the *San Francisco Bulletin*:

His right hand has lost none of its cunning. He possesses the same marvelous strength yet delicacy of touch— the same control of his instrument, the same faculty of throwing his whole soul into the passion of the music. After hearing other accomplished musicians, we are more than impressed with Ole Bull's greatness. He stands alone.

Next, he proceeded to Madison, Wisc., where the family of Joseph G. Thorp, a wealthy lumberman and state senator, hosted him at the family mansion on Lake Mendota. With the encouragement of the senator's shrewd and strong-willed wife, Amelia, the 60-year-old Bull took a romantic interest in the Thorps' 20-year-old daughter, Sara.

A black-haired, pensive woman, Sara Thorp had been sheltered by her parents while she developed her own considerable skills as a pianist. Although three times her age, Bull was still a distinguished-looking, compelling figure, with handsome features and a muscular body. He remained particularly attractive to the opposite sex, as noted by Longfellow, who wrote that whenever Bull spoke to a woman, "you would think he was presenting her with a bouquet."

Joseph Thorp disapproved of the sudden romance between his daughter and the aging Norwegian musician. Nevertheless, Bull, a widower for eight years, became enamored with Sara.

"My prayer to the almighty is embodied in the whisper, 'Sara.' My music, my ambition, my love of country, my destiny, my future country, my whole trust hereafter and forever is Sara," he penned to her in a letter mailed from Baltimore.

When Bull finished his spring tour and arrived in New York, ready to sail back to Norway, Sara Thorp and her mother were on the steamer *Russia* to join him. James Reymert, a Norwegian banker who tended to Bull's financial affairs, and New York Philharmonic President Dr. Robert Doremus organized a festive send-off in the New York Harbor. "So thoroughly good and noble, democratic and straightforward as Ole Bull is, he has made millions of friends," the *New York Democrat* reported. "No foreigner has won our hearts as has Ole Bull."

A silken flag of Norwegian colors, with the U.S. flag inserted in the upper staff section, was presented by Dr. Doremus. Bull would later carry the flag during Norwegian Constitution Day processions and fly it at his home on special occasions.

"The company waved together their regrets and their farewells; and the form of the fine old gentleman, bare-headed and swinging his hat, was seen as long as forms could be distinguished in the distance," the *New York Tribune* reported.

The Thorps were Bull's guests at Valestrand for several weeks. Mortimer Smith's book described the experience as idyllic, "walking and sailing around the numerous little islands, riding on Ole's horses;

the evenings they would spend in the music room, Ole playing Norwegian airs to Sara's expert piano accompaniment."

During this period, Sara Thorp became pregnant with Ole Bull's child. Amelia Thorp was soon telling all that Ole and Sara had been married in a "quiet ceremony" at Christiania, and that their vows would be renewed to conform to U.S. marital law later in the year. To admit to an out-of-wedlock pregnancy in that Victorian era would have created a scandal.

Bull spent most of his time in Christiania and at Valestrand, still disappointed by the Norwegian government's attitude, as well as the public's lukewarm response to his mission of preserving and promoting their unique artistic and musical traditions. He was as anxious as the Thorps to return to the U.S. Upon their arrival in Madison, Amelia Thorp arranged for a quiet marriage ceremony before a local pastor, followed by a gala reception at the Thorps' mansion on Sept. 22.

Soon after their child, Olea Sara Bull, arrived on March 4, 1871, the Bulls temporarily moved into a home at West Lebanon, Maine, ostensibly because the Thorps believed the climate there would be better for the baby girl's health. This house had belonged to Mrs. Abbie Shapleigh, a friend of the Thorps who stayed there as well, probably keeping tabs on Ole and Sara. Ole showed Sara another side of life. She flowered into a forceful, artistic woman in her own right, not inclined to bow to unreasonable pressure from her parents or anyone else.

Ole was treated as a celebrity in the small community as he mingled with the locals. He enjoyed gathering around the cracker barrel at the village store and chatting with townspeople about music, politics and other interests. At his home, he introduced them to billiards, a game to which he was passionately devoted. Bull also enjoyed playing his violin at church services and informal gatherings.

Relations with the Thorps were strained, as explained by Bull biographer Mortimer Smith in this summary:

Their whole attitude towards life was strange and repugnant to him, and for a long time he struggled against it with all the force he could command. He was an impulsive, careless soul who throughout his life had moved among people of easy tolerance, people who accepted one's actions and one's opinions without question, and who never sat in moral judgment on others.

He was an artist, and he had lived in a world peopled with artists or those who appreciated the freedom and unrestraint of artistic temperament. The Thorps, on the other hand, were definitely bourgeois; they had standards and a very definite code of behavior, and they knew the correct attitude toward every problem under the sun. It was only natural that when such an unorthodox soul as Ole Bull became a member of the family, they should attempt to covert him.

Ole resisted them at first with considerable vigor, but in the end they—and old age—conquered, or at least achieved a fairly impressive victory. Nothing and nobody could entirely quell that tempestuous nature, but it was softened a little here and modified there, until the Thorps could be reasonably sure that their distinguished son-in-law would not say or do anything too shocking for the sensitive feelings of their eminently correct friends. The Ole Bull who figures largely in American memoirs of the 1870s—a white-haired, saintly old man exuding sweetness and light—is not the essential Ole Bull; he is an Ole Bull tamed by his wife's family.

Bull appeared content to live out the final years of his life as a Norwegian-American in the truest sense, with loyalties to—and appreciation of—both nations. His friendship with Rasmus B. Anderson, a young Scandinavian language instructor at the University of Wisconsin, led to a concert by Bull in the General Assembly chamber of the State Capitol to raise money for an extensive Norwegian book collection at the university. Bull was impressed with Anderson's devotion to Scandinavian culture and his commitment to making Americans who shared his national background conscious and proud of their heritage.

Bull and Anderson then set off on the White Star steam *Atlantic* in

June 1872 for Christiania to select and purchase the books. Although Sara and young Olea stayed behind in Madison, Joseph Thorp and his son, Joseph Jr., also boarded the *Atlantic*, perhaps to keep their eyes on Ole.

During this visit to Norway, Bull made arrangements for the purchase of Lysoen ("the island of light"), a 170-acre North Sea island lying 20 miles south of Bergen. The island consisted almost exclusively of forestland that rose to a peak with an unobstructed view of the coastal mountains and the ocean. Bull engaged an architect to develop plans for a home to be built on the island, incorporating the native architecture of many nations he had visited.

The home, now a tourist attraction, combines simple Norwegian peasant and "stave church" with Moorish, Russian and a generous touch of Victorian gingerbread. The unusual carvings and turned pillars reflect Bull's own complex personality. Its grand music room is high, with elaborately carved columns cut out of pine taken from the island itself.

During their voyage, Anderson persuaded Bull to throw his influence behind a plan to have a monument erected in Boston to honor Leif Ericson, son of Eric the Red, a Norwegian. Bull, who ardently championed Ericson over Columbus as the original discoverer of America, believed the statue would as much honor the Vikings' adventurous spirit as Ericson himself. Anderson, in return, agreed to teach Norwegian to Sara. To raise money for the monument and satisfy the Thorps, Bull returned to the concert stage. Some of his performances, such as those in the Norwegian villages of Wisconsin, Minnesota and Iowa, featured Sara Bull as accompanist and Rasmus Anderson as speaker. Bull also appeared in Boston, New Orleans, Chicago and other major cities, with his concerts well received and financially rewarding.

Bull believed that Norwegians should also contribute to the fund, so he set off on a concert tour in Norway, accompanied by Sara and her family, using the new home at Lysoen as his base. These 1873 performances were particularly significant, because Edvard Grieg served as Bull's accompanist while Bjornstjerne Bjornson appeared as a speaker.

Anderson further promoted the cause by publishing a controversial and popular book entitled, "America Not Discovered by Columbus."

Relations between Bull and the Thorps worsened in 1874, culminating with the return of the whole Thorp family, including Sara and Olea, to Wisconsin in May. Meanwhile, Ole traveled to Rome to socialize with Bjornson, who took great delight in Bull's tales of the conflicts between himself and the Thorps. He then returned to Lysoen to work on the grounds and settle in for the winter.

Still separated from his wife and child, Bull scheduled concerts in Norway, Sweden, Denmark and Germany. In most cities, he was received with more acclaim than ever. He moved on to Egypt, where he honored a promise he had made to King Oscar II of Sweden by climbing to the summit of the Cheops Pyramid on his 66th birthday to perform "Herd Girl's Sunday."

After stops in Switzerland, Italy and Germany, he arrived in Bergen to join Edvard Grieg for a National Stage of Bergen fund-raiser on the national holiday, May 17, 1876. Although Grieg's reputation would grow to exceed that of Bull, he never lost his respect for his mentor. Mortimer Smith wrote:

Their relationship was like that of a father and son, marked by genuine understanding and affection. As a young boy, Grieg's great hero was Ole Bull, and he never wholly lost the attitude of hero worship as he grew older. Grieg, indeed, owed much to Ole Bull, a debt he always freely acknowledged. Bull was not only the first to recognize the potential genius of the 'Chopin of the North,' but was perhaps the most important single factor in determining the direction Grieg's music was to take.

The one missing ingredient in his life was Sara, who resisted her husband's many pleas for her to return until she finally consented in spring 1876, sailing to Lysoen to join him. She never left Ole's side again. Sara even persuaded Bull to accompany her back to the U.S. later that year, where he reconciled with the Thorps.

With Sara in charge of his scheduling and finances, Bull continued to perform and renewed his efforts on behalf of the Leif Ericson monument. One of several concerts in Boston was organized as a monument fund-raiser. Performances arranged by Maurice Strakosch, with American singer Emma Thursby as soloist, thrilled audiences in New York.

Ole granted a long interview to a *New York Herald* reporter, providing colorful descriptions of his early career, his relationships with Paganini, Chopin, Ernst and other greats, and his playful interaction with European royalty. He also detailed his strong dislike for the music of Richard Wagner: "We have only to listen to the melodies of Mozart, Rossini, Handel and Bach to feel that there is no comparison between their beautiful works and the monstrosities of the Wagner school . . . A person who comes out of Wagner's concert is not to be trusted. There is murder in that music and something which appeals to the lower passions. It makes honest people sick."

Perhaps enjoying the spotlight, Bull detailed certain developments in his life that were either exaggerated or complete fiction. He discussed a duel with another musician in Germany, during which he supposedly killed his adversary and fled to avoid prosecution. Bull also told of a time he was robbed of all he owned, including his favorite violin, while in Paris. Driven to despair, Bull continued, he attempted suicide by jumping into the Seine River, only to be rescued.

Bull's Oleana experience merited only one sentence: "I had some unfortunate experience in attempting to establish a colony of my countrymen in Pennsylvania on account of having fallen into the hands of swindlers, who sold me land to which they had no title."

The Bulls returned to Lysoen for a quiet summer in 1877. They later toured several European cities, with Ole renewing acquaintances and keeping to a relaxed concert schedule, culminating with Bull's final Bergen performance in August 1878. They returned to the U.S., where Bull resumed his appearances with Maurice Strakosch and Emma Thursby, amassing a small fortune. Rasmus Anderson joined the tour to promote the Ericson monument and spend time with Bull. Anderson wrote:

Bull is in fine shape. He does not need to give concerts. He has an annual income of 4,000 dollars as long as he lives and Mrs. Bull has 5,000 a year. That he still gives concerts has several reasons. For one thing he is not happy unless he is playing in public, and for another his concerts are so well paid that it is not easy to resist the temptation. For his concerts this winter he has gotten 500 dollars and all expenses . . . He is daily invited as a guest by the most famous and respected men. I am sorry to say it, but I think it true that Ole Bull meets more true cordiality and appreciation here than in Norway.

Bull was back at Lysoen in 1879. A disease later diagnosed as stomach cancer was beginning to sap his strength and endurance. Ole participated in the Constitution Day parade in Bergen, met up with Edvard Grieg and Hardanger fiddler Ole Mosafinn at Lofthus and helped Bergensers host a visit by King Oscar II. Then he and Sara prepared to return to America.

"On the last day and evening every part of the island was visited," Sara recalled. "It was in truth a farewell, and it now seems as if the last lingering looks rested with more than wonted tenderness on the spot he so loved; for it was the last time his foot pressed the soil, as on his next return he was borne in the arms of others to his home."

For a time, he settled in at Cambridge, Mass., spending many hours with Longfellow and James Fields. On Jan. 29, 1880, Bull was joined on stage in Boston by Ralph Waldo Emerson and Oliver Wendell Holmes to aid the Old South Preservation Fund. During a party at Fields' home in April, Bull spoke extensively with Mark Twain, who later wrote: "What a lovable people the Bulls are— both of them . . . If Ole Bull had been born without arms, what a rank he would have taken among the poets because it is IN him and if he couldn't violin it out, he would talk it out, since of course it would have to come out."

His tour continued through May, concluding at Chicago's Grand

Central Music Hall, where Ole stepped onto the stage for the final time. A flare-up developed between the Bulls and the Thorps, who wanted Ole and Sara to remain in Wisconsin so Bull could receive medical care. The Bulls nevertheless left for Europe on June 30. Ole fell gravely ill, but survived the trip to Liverpool. After resting for several days under a physician's care, Bull insisted upon crossing the North Sea to Bergen and on to Lysoen. He seemed to rally briefly after he arrived at the island. Among his visitors in his final days was his daughter, Felicie Ingier.

Sara remained by her husband's bedside, keeping vigil as his condition worsened. "For forty years and more Bull had been one of the great national heroes, not strictly as a musical figure, but as a symbol of modest little Norway's claim to fame in the world at large, and now his imminent death became a subject of universal concern," Mortimer Smith wrote.

On Aug. 17, 1880, he asked Sara to play Mozart's "Requiem" on their organ in the music hall. Its sullen tones echoed through the house as she performed the piece several times. At quarter past noon, Ole Bull drew his last breath. Sara described the end: "He gave the sweet assurance that life had been precious to him, and the dear smile lighted the way for all, as he passed beyond."

A service was held in the music hall at the Lysoen home, where Grieg performed a prelude on the organ. Bull's body was then carried by steamer to the Bergen Harbor, where a convoy of vessels joined in the procession. Guns were sounded and most of the townspeople lined the shore for the official day of mourning.

At the cemetery, Bjornstjerne Bjornson delivered a stirring eulogy:

When he first appeared among us, we were a poor, small nation with glorious traditions of earlier times, starting afresh with longings not soon to be realized, longings for which we were sometimes mocked . . . We had been newly bought and sold, and what little liberty we had presumed to seize gave us no security, but much concern. But a young generation came, nourished on freedom, and without the fear and prudence of their elders, but with more of defiance and anger. They lived in the morning of freedom and honor, and in this dawn came Ole Bull's tones like the first rays of sun over the mountaintops.

Older men have told you of the giant form which suddenly stood forth in the highest places, before kings and the most cultured, and played with a wild power, possessed by only one man before, but in Ole Bull more original, more humanly sympathetic— a power for the first time Norse.

When they read how he stood and sang Norwegian melodies from his violin to other nations, we felt that they were one with us while they were moved to laughter and tears as they caught glimpses of our people and grand, beautiful nature; thus, one may understand the confidence, the faith, the pride he awakened . . . He gave us self-respect, the greatest gift possible at that time. This is Ole Bull's undying honor; this is the supreme accomplishment of his life . . .

The criticism has been made that Ole Bull has failed in not leaving behind him great musical works. This is unjust. A man that could so fully give what he at times gave us could not do more . . . Always before we have spoken in Ole Bull's honor we have closed with a, "Long live Ole Bull!" This we may never say again— though dead to us he is not. He will be with us when we return to our homes.

The diminutive Edvard Grieg, who would carry the tradition of Norwegian music to new heights, stepped forward to lay a laurel wreath on the coffin, hailing Bull for "planting a seed which shall spring up in the future and for which coming celebrations shall bless thee."

After the body had been lowered into the grave and relatives had departed, there was one final tribute paid to Ole Bull. Hundreds of Norwegians from far and near, many of them peasants and poor farmers, filed past the gravesite, covering the coffin with pine boughs, ferns and flowers.

Epilogue

Private holdings in and around Oleana have changed hands many times over the years. The land was a gold mine for timber interests who denuded the hillsides in the 1890-1915 era and then moved on, abandoning the Potter County property and allowing the state to acquire it for nonpayment of taxes.

Evergreens and other species that generated a considerable amount of wealth for the lumber barons are gone, but many varieties of deciduous trees have grown in their place. These give the Kettle Creek valley a new kind of beauty.

As the Norwegians were moving out, the Germans were moving in. William Radde, a wealthy publisher and promoter from New York City, formed the "Pennsylvania Farm and Land Association." Its purpose was the purchase of 90,000 acres to be divided into 25-acre farms, with the village of Germania in Abbott Township, a few miles northeast of the New Bergen settlement, as its hub.

Radde ended up buying most of the land himself and the "association" served little purpose. He also acquired the holdings of Norwegian and Danish settlers who remained at the Ole Bull colony in New Bergen (Cartee Camp) in late 1855. Most of the Scandinavians used the money to cover traveling expenses to Wisconsin.

By then, Dr. Charles Meine and his associates had arrived in Abbott Township. Along with Radde, they supervised the orderly development of the Germania area. The scenario was a familiar one— Germans who arrived in the late 1850s were dismayed to learn that the setting was not nearly as idyllic as the promoters had claimed. Acreage that was depicted as rolling hills and flat land with soils conducive to farming actually consisted of steep forested slopes. Under strong leadership, Germania did grow to become a thriving community.

Dr. Meine, who studied medicine in his native Germany, was still working as the town doctor and postmaster in Germania at the turn of the century when he was interviewed by Torstein Jahr. Meine had in his possession the so-called "Ole Bull Bible," a German Bible in pictures (1686), which Ole Bull presented to the colony. That Bible was eventually donated to the Potter County Historical Society by Meine's descendants.

Although he never met Bull, Dr. Meine was familiar with many of the settlers and described what he encountered upon his arrival in the Kettle Creek valley:

When we came to Potter in October 1855, between 18 and 20 Norwegian and Danish families were already here. A Sunday walk around town to get some bread could not find anything except for some oatmeal cookies. At that time, there were lots of fish and wild animals in the woods. Wolves and other dangerous animals were also around.

The poor colonists had a tough time. They came from a cold and mountain-rich country, but did not understand how to use the land here. They cut down the trees, but started also to dig up the roots, which was slow and tiresome work.

Writers, researchers and historians have reached a wide variety of conclusions about the Oleana— its significance, the causes of its failure and the lessons that can be learned from the experience. The 20/20 vision that hindsight provides often seems unflattering to Ole Bull, just as his own pleas for sympathy or claims of victimization may ring hollow with some.

The Ole Bull Colony

Torstein Jahr, whose expertise on Scandinavia served him well during a career with the Library of Congress from 1901 to 1928, preserved for historians a wide variety of material on the Oleana experience.

His education, combined with considerable research and exclusive interviews with colonists and their descendants, gave Jahr insight that he shared through the periodical *Symra* almost a century ago:

It was but natural that a plan to found a colony of his countrymen should appeal very strongly to the bighearted Ole Bull. He felt assured that emigration to the new world could not be checked. America became the promised land for all who were tired of Europe and hungered for change and excitement.

Jonas Lie had said about Ole Bull's project: "It was a brilliant plan. A politician or a financier would probably have envied him the plan, but such a one would probably have seen to it that the practical arrangements were made by somebody other than Ole Bull."

Of all his rather numerous illusions or visionary plans, this one was the most far-reaching. As a passing chapter in his life's history and as a sort of interlude in the history of Norwegian immigration to America, it cannot be passed by. Every scrap of detail we are able to collect is of such interest and importance that it is worth preserving.

Many Norwegians had heard of about Oleana, but only a few are able to give its geographical position and there may be a reason for this. For most of us, this name plays the same part as El Dorado, Utopia, or the lost Atlantis, places that are not found on any map. It is a difficult task to ask yourself what would be the result if this or that happened or did not happen.

But a last remark should be mentioned. A friend of mine wrote: "Had Oleana been successful, could he have given so much? Would not material interest have developed less the man to whom suffering a disappointment meant greater effort, deeper belief in humanity when individuals failed him, and a firmer grip upon the task he was himself set to perform?"

A modern-day version of Torstein Jahr is Paul Engelstad, a diplomatic relations officer for the U.S. State Department and a writer and lecturer on Ole Bull. For many years, he has retraced Bull's footsteps in Norway and the United States and continues to broaden his perspective:

Ole Bull was a man of many contradictions— one minute almost superhuman and then falling to great depths. That's what makes him so fascinating as a character. He was able to use his great charm to manipulate others, and capable of turning on those who loved him with great disregard for the outcome. But curiously, he seemed to feel a great sense of hurt when treated in a like manner by those from whom he sought approval. What a life of highs and lows; successes and failures!

From the Potter County perspective, W. W. Thompson and Dr. George Donehoo concluded that Ole Bull's colony was doomed from the start. Each of these men courageously shared his views with the public, risking the ire of the many who preferred to believe that Bull was a victim of others' greed and deceit, and that all of the colonists were ambitious and motivated by a strong sense of community.

Thompson summarized his findings as follows:

Ole Bull had made many promises that could not be kept. There was much complaint because he did not visit the colony. The men had only to work for the colony and for this they received some store pay, but little or no money. They were dissatisfied and their work as a whole was poor indeed. Perhaps if there had been an effort to keep the promises and the men were promptly paid a reasonable wage, things would have been different.

The men were given free board, instead of being compelled to pay board. This kind of prosperity did not make for good work with a considerable portion of the men. There were some notable exceptions . . . Funds were not sufficient and complaints from the colonists were more than aplenty. The cry was for Ole Bull, who came not, and for pay that was not forthcoming.

Dr. Donehoo, founder of the Potter County Historical Society, delivered an even harsher and more unflattering judgment of the colonists in a 1920 address:

Anyone familiar with the conditions which these colonists had to face in this then-almost unbroken wilderness, far distant from any base of supplies and with little money and no business management, can realize that the colony was doomed to failure from the day it started.

Ole Bull did not see this entire valley and all of these mountains locked up by the snow king from the commencement of winter until spring. He did not realize that the people who were coming into these unbroken wilds would have to face a long winter in hastily erected huts where the temperature would drop to 40 degrees below zero and hover about zero for weeks at a time.

To add to the discontent and dissatisfaction of these colonists, the management of affairs was in such a state that any such enterprise, even in entirely different conditions, would have failed. The men were fed, whether they worked or not. And when they discovered that they would be provided for without effort, they ceased all effort. They made no attempt to build houses for themselves, but simply planned to get out of the place as soon as they could get enough money to do so.

The hardy pioneers who came into the wilderness, single-handed with nothing but ax and rifle, won in the conflicts with the grim hardships of nature, while these colonists failed because they did not have to work or starve to death. The mountains were filled with great stores of game and fish, which were left untouched because the "company" would feed them with the meager provisions which were brought on horseback or in wagon from Coudersport and Jersey Shore.

The men had nothing to do, so they grumbled and complained at their sad condition. Charges of every sort against Ole Bull were made and discussed . . . Robert Hamilton had to face the fight right here, listening to complaints of the colonists, advising sensible methods of management which were unheeded, until he finally resigned.

Lawsuits filed after the colony's collapse lingered for several years. Among them was surveyor Robert Hamilton's claim against Bull, which was settled through the public sale of Bull's surveying tools, the proceeds going to Hamilton.

Another associate of Bull at Oleana, John F. Cowan, remained in Williamsport, Pa., where he was identified with many business activities. He became a stockholder in West Branch Bank and was active in promoting the Sunbury and Erie Railroad, now a part of the Pennsylvania Railroad system.

Cowan was recalled by townspeople as a sharp dresser and lavish spender, living in great style for the era, and he made considerable money in land speculation. Some years after the Ole Bull episode, in the list of lands advertised for sale for taxes in Potter County, he was the reputed owner of 103 tracts, most of them for full warrants of 900 to 1,000 acres. Cowan ended up in New York during the Civil War and died there.

Emigrant agent John Nathaniel Holfeldt relocated to Canada after the Oleana colony collapse. He returned to Norway in 1863, settling in Stavanger, and died prematurely later that same year on a recreation trip to the South.

Pastor Jacob Aall Otteson became one of the founders of the Lutheran Synod in America, serving as a pastor in Manitowec and Koshkonong, Wisc., as well as Decorah, Iowa. He also was a magazine editor in Madison and Decorah from 1861 to 1868. He died at Decorah in 1904.

Only two of Ole and Felicie Bull's six children outlived him. Eleonore Felicie married Dr. Christoffer Ingier in Norway. They had six children. She died in 1923 at Christiania. Alexander became a violinist, living much of his life in America. He died at Christiania in 1914. Lucie married attorney Peter Jacob Homann and died less than a year later in 1869.

Newspapers of the era contained colorful accounts of Sara Bull's latter years. She became fascinated with an eastern cult known as "Raja Yogi," signifying at that time "the path to wisdom, promising eternal youth, health and long life."

Sara Bull's home in Cambridge and summer home at Green Acres, Maine, were headquarters for not only the intellectual society and for leaders of social causes, but also for "the faithful." The latter held a meditation chamber with lighted candles and burning incense and other "Oriental trappings," as the newspaper called them.

Sara's death after a long illness at Cambridge, Mass., on Jan. 18, 1911, revealed that she had been a convert to the Vendanta philosophy espoused by the Swami Vivekananda, and had left the Bull fortune to this group.

The Bulls' daughter, Mrs. Olea Bull Vaughan, contested her mother's will, resulting in a Probate Court hearing in Alfred, Maine, during which Sara's bizarre behavior and unconventional beliefs were described by witnesses. As testimony continued, the presiding judge closed the proceedings to the public, eventually returning to open court to announce that Sara Bull's will would be set aside because of "mental incapacitation and undue influence."

The same day that the court ruled in her favor, in July 1911, Olea Bull Vaughan died of tuberculosis. The Lysoen Island home became the possession of Sylvea Bull Curtis, Olea's daughter.

On May 21, 1974, in the presence of the Royal Family and more than 100 guests, Sylvea Bull Curtis conveyed Lysoen to the Norwegian Society for the Protection of Ancient Monuments. The home, now a well-maintained tourist attraction and memorial to Ole and Sara Bull, is the setting for public recitals each summer and is visited by thousands people each year.

A *Philadelphia Inquirer* newspaper reporter paid a visit to the villages of Ole Bull's colony some 35 years after the colony's rise and fall. Excerpts of his report give the reader a glimpse of the area just before the lumber barons moved in:

Oleana

Up among the forest-covered mountains of the most desolate portion of Pennsylvania, far from civilization, are three small villages, or rather the remains of them. The houses built by the settlers have many of them tumbled down; the clearings made have become overgrown with scrub, oaks and bushes, and the inhabitants have sought homes elsewhere.

The villages were never large except in name, and now they look very small and dilapidated. The houses were built in a strange, foreign sort of style, with windows and porches of the most unaccountable shapes in the most unexpected places. Many of them are sort of cross between a Swiss chalet and an Indian bungalow, and a visitor can easily make himself believe he is in any place but America, so little like home do the houses look. The steep roofs and narrow, upstairs porches are like those of the houses the colonists left behind in Norway, and would be stranger still were there any dwellings of the American style with which to compare them; but this settlement is far away from any other.

Here among the mountains the great musician spent a year, and his friends say that the bitterest disappointment of his life was the awaking from the dream of a great colony in the wilderness.

Leaving Coudersport in an old-fashioned buckboard wagon, New Bergen is the first settlement reached. The post office, which is the principal building, is a small one- and one-half story structure which is used for a hotel, courthouse, hospital or auction hall, as necessity demands. The village, if village it may be called, was originally located in the little valley occupied by the post office alone, but it was soon moved to the hill nearby, probably to escape the spring floods which every year pour through the little valley, making a clean sweep. Half a dozen or more tumble-down dwelling houses are scattered on the steep hillside, and with the basement stories and high porches, they look like a group of children's block houses, which a gust of wind might overthrow.

A short distance from New Bergen is Oleana, which was to have been the capital city of the new territory Ole Bull proposed to govern. Now there is little left except three or four houses, the hotel and one store. The hotel is kept by a pleasant, intelligent and thrifty looking Norwegian who says it was built by Ole Bull, who at one time had a music hall attached to it, where he treated the settlers to such music as he never gave elsewhere. The hall has been torn down for firewood.

Two miles below Oleana, after a drive up over the cool green mountains, we reach New Norway, the last of these settlements. If we except one small house it is safe to say that New Norway is entirely gone, with nothing left behind but the cleared plain and here and there the moss-grown stone foundations of an old house long since rotted away. The village and villagers are gone, but even now, looking at the level, grass-grown plain, one can imagine that it must have been a pretty place with green lawns and fine yards, for the ground is rich and moist, bearing luxuriant grass in even the driest weather.

Even after his death, Ole Bull remained a unifying force for Norwegian-Americans. They rallied behind a plan to erect a monument to Bull in Minneapolis's Loring Park. A concert featuring Alexander Bull on violin, accompanied by Sara Bull on piano, raised money to help finance the monument. More than 6,000 people turned out at the Minnesota Exposition Building on May 17, 1896, for the unveiling of a plaster model of the Ole Bull statue— possibly the largest gathering of Norwegians under one roof in America up to that time.

Once the model was cast into bronze, it was transported to Minneapolis for a dedication ceremony on May 17, 1897. This time, an estimated 25,000 people were in attendance. Immediately after the unveiling, Alexander Bull performed a selection on one of his late father's violins. Following the dedication, Alexander placed at the base of the statue a wreath of heather, Bull's favorite flower, made by Ole and Sara Bull's daughter, Eleonore Felicie Ingier. Each May 17, Norwegian-Americans gather at the Bull statue to pay tribute to their homeland and the artist who inspired so many of their ancestors.

Two Ole Bull statues are prominently displayed in his birthplace. One was created in 1901 by sculptor Stephan Sinding and is located in a busy downtown area. The other, by Ambrosia Tonnesen, greets visitors to the auditorium of the Bergen Theater.

Several prominent institutions in the U.S. have been established for the preservation and research of the history and culture of Norwegian America. Among them are the Norwegian-American Historical Association, with headquarters and archives at St. Olaf College in Northfield, Minn; the Vesterheim Norwegian-American Museum at Luther College in Decorah, Iowa; and the Nordic Heritage Museum in Seattle, Wash.

The Norwegian Immigration Association was formed to develop an exhibit honoring the Norwegian immigrants to the New York area. This display, "Norwegians in New York, 1825 to 2000: Builders of City, Community and Culture," debuted at the Ellis Island Museum and has since found a permanent home at the Norwegian Christian Home and Health Center in Brooklyn, N.Y.

Heritage organizations such as the Sons of Norway are preserving Norwegian cultural traditions in their general activities and through their support of museums, folk craft exhibitions, genealogical research and festivals.

In Norway, the Norwegian Emigrant Museum and Research Center at Stange, near Hamar, and emigration centers in Stavanger and Bergen complement the U.S. endeavors.

Bull's Norwegian Theater at Bergen has been reconstructed as the National Stage in Bergen. The Norwegian Music Academy of which he dreamed was realized after his death when a music conservatory was founded in Oslo.

In 1973, the Ole Bull Academy opened in Voss, Norway. Its special emphasis is Norwegian folk music, dancing and folktales.

The house where Ole Bull was born on Strandgaten Street in Bergen was destroyed by fire in 1916. The pharmacy, Svaneapoteket (Swan Pharmacy), still exists at the same site.

The home at Valestrand is still standing, much of it unchanged from the days of its occupancy by the Bulls. Alexander Bull inherited the property, then turned it over to his sister Eleonore Felicie. Only one of her children, daughter Lucie Jonassen, had children of her own. Her daughter Anne Margrete married opera singer Arne Hendriksen. Their son, Knut Hendriksen, Ole's Bull's great great grandson, now maintains the Valestrand home as private residence.

Many of those white hats that Bull sent for the colonists ended up in the hands of Henry Andresen, who sold them for a modest profit many years after the colony's collapse. These hats could occasionally be seen being worn by local lumberjacks, in mockery of Ole Bull.

In July 1920, the Potter County Historical Society and Pennsylvania Historical Commission sponsored a "pilgrimage" to the Oleana/New Norway area to recall the memory of Ole Bull and the colonists. This was a major event, well-promoted and attended by at least 2,000 people. Forest Commissioner Gifford Pinchot, a noted conservationist, and Governor William Sproul were among the speakers.

Dr. Will George Butler of Mansfield, Pa., author of many musical compositions and a talented violinist, performed his "Visions of Oleana," as well as a Beethoven sonata reputed to be one of Ole Bull's favorites. The Butler piece was performed on numerous occasions by John Philip Sousa's band.

John H. Chatham of McElhattan, Pa., recited a lengthy, lyrical poem he wrote for the occasion. An excerpt from his "Ode to Ole Bull":

And here around his Lyso Spring,
He made the hills with music ring.
Its echoes hushed in wood and glen,
Still vibrate in the hearts of men,
And wake to ecstasy or tear,
The living souls assembled here.

Bull's Stradivarius is now encased at the Smithsonian's Museum of American History. It may be the instrument Bull purchased in Budapest in the 1840s, reputed to have been custom-made for Spanish King Philip VII in 1687. During the Christmas season in 1999, Norway's greatest living violinist, Arve Tellefsen, performed "Herd Girl's Sunday" and "A Mother's Prayer" on the instrument during a visit to the museum.

Later that year, during a private tour of the area where Bull established his Oleana/New Norway colony, Tellefsen performed several of Bull's original compositions, much to the delight of a small group of listeners. The setting was Ole Bull State Park, a fitting memorial to the musician established in portions of the former New Norway and Valhalla communities. There are campsites, picnic grounds, cooking arches, a rental cabin and other conveniences for the thousands of visitors who visit the park year-'round. The Ole Bull Memorial Planting, now a forest of tall white pine trees, surrounds the park's southern entrance.

Visitors to the park can climb the short "Castle Vista Trail" to the shelf of Nordjenskald Mountain, where they can look upon the few remaining portions of the cabin's stone foundation and look out over the rolling hills of what was once the vast domain of Ole Bull.

Bibliography

Hundreds of references were used in the development of this book, ranging from four major biographical works on Ole Bull to tattered newspaper clippings and hand-scrawled notes dating back to the middle of the 19th century. It is impossible to list each reference source, since in some cases the origins of a document are unclear. The following bibliography represents a good faith effort to recognize every identifiable source of information for this work.

Abell, Arthur M. "Famous Violinists of the Past, VII: Ole Bull." *Musical Courier*, New York, N.Y., 1908.

Amerika, Ole Bull og det nye Norge. Bergen, Norway, 1852.

Andersen, Hans Christian. "An Episode in Ole Bull's Life." *Vestlandske Tidende*, September 1839.

Anderson, Rasmus B. *Life Story*, Madison, Wisc., 1915.

Arctander, John W. "Ole Bull." *Skandinaven*, May 26, 1887, Chicago, Ill.

Asbjornsen, Peter Christen and Moe, Jorgen. "Norwegian Folk Tales," New York, N.Y., 1982.

Barton, Albert O. "Ole Bull and his Wisconsin Contacts." *Wisconsin Magazine of History* 7, 1924.

Beebe, Victor L. *History of Potter County*, Potter County Historical

Society, Coudersport Pa., 1934.

Beers, J.H. *History of the Counties of McKean, Elk, Cameron and Potter, Pennsylvania.* J.H. Beers and Company, Chicago, Ill., 1890.

Bergland, Betty. "Norwegian Immigrants and 'Indianerne' in the Landtaking, 1838-1862." Financed by Fulbright Research Grant, 1998-1999.

Bergsagel, John. "Ole Bull." Stanley Sadie, ed., *The New Grove Dictionary of Music and Musicians,* London, 1980.

Bjork, Kenneth O. *West of the Great Divide: Norwegian Migration to the Pacific Coast, 1847-1893.* Norwegian-American Historical Assn., Northfield, Minn., 1958.

Blegen, Theodore C. *Norwegian Migration to America 1825-1860,* Arno Press, New York, N.Y., 1969.

Blegen, Theodore C. *Norwegian Migration to America, The American Transition.* Norwegian-American Historical Assn., Northfield, Minn., 1940.

Blegen, Theodore C., and Ruud, Martin S. *Norwegian Songs and Ballads.* University of Minnesota, 1936.

Bo, Erling. "Christianity in Norway." *Nytt fra Norge* for the Ministry of Foreign Affairs, 1995.

Bowen, Eli. *The Pictorial Sketch-book of Pennsylvania.* Second edition. Philadelphia, Pa., 1853.

Brig Incognito, *100 Years of Emigrant Ships from Norway.* Translated by Trond Austheim, September 1999.

Bull, Jens. *Den Tronserske Slekt Bull.* Oslo, Norway, 1937.

Bull, Sara C. *Ole Bull: A Memoir,* Boston and New York, 1882.

Buraas, Anders. "Ole Bull: Violinist and Colonizer." *Scanorama,* Stockholm, Sweden, June/July 1976.

Buslett, Ole A. *The Fifteenth Regiment, Wisconsin Volunteers.* Decorah, Iowa, 1895

Calmeyer, Bengt. "Norwegian Theatre— More Than Just Ibsen." Ministry of Foreign Affairs, Norway, 1996.

Chatham, John H. "Ode to Ole Bull." *Potter County Journal,*

Coudersport, Pa., Aug. 25, 1920.

Child, Lydia Maria. *Letters from New York.* New York, N.Y., 1846.

Civil War Compiled Military Service Records. Office of Adjutant General of the United States, Washington, D.C.

Cleven, Harry T. "The Fifteenth Wisconsin Regiment in the American Civil War."

Cooke, George Willis. "Ole Bull's First Appearances in America." Music II, November 1896 to April 1897.

Cornelius, James M. *The Norwegian Americans.* Chelsea House Publishers, New York, N.Y., 1989.

Currin, Robert K. "Potter County: At the Edge of the Forest." *Pennsylvania Heritage*, Spring 1989.

Dagre, Tor. "The History of Norway." *Nytt fra Norge*, Oslo, Norway.

Doremus, Dr. R. Ogden. "Edwin Booth and Ole Bull." *The Critic*, New Rochelle, N.Y., March 1906.

Dwight, John Sullivan. "Ole Bull and his Colony." *Dwight's Journal of Music,* May 1853.

Egle, William H. *An Illustrated History of the Commonwealth of Pennsylvania.* W.C. Goodrich, Harrisburg, Pa.

Emigranten, Norwegian-American newspaper. Various articles.

Engelstad, Paul. "Mr. Bull Goes to Washington." An essay. December 1999.

Espeland, Velle. "Folk Music." Internet, 2001.

Finck, Henry T. "Masters of the Violin." *The Mentor,* New York, N.Y., 1916.

Follesdal, John. "Ancestors from Norway." Internet, 2001

Gay, Cecile. *Ole Bull: Violiniste Norvegien.* Paris, France, 1881.

Gjerset, Knut, and Hektoen, Ludvig. "Health Conditions and the Practice of Medicine Among Early Norwegian Settlers, 1825-1865." Norwegian-American Historical Assn., Northfield, Minn.

Glassmire, Samuel H. "Ole Bull's History." *Potter County Journal*, Coudersport, Pa., Aug. 11, 1920.

Goldschmidt, Meir. "A Norwegian Musician." *Cornhill Magazine*, April 1862.

Grinde, Nils. *A History of Norwegian Music*. Trans. and ed. by William H. Halverson and Leland B. Sateren, Lincoln, Neb., 1991.

Haaeim, Sjur Jorgensen. *Information on Conditions in North America*. Christiania, Norway, 1842.

Haarklou, Johannes. "The Life of Ole Bull." *Music*, December 1901.

Hanslick, Eduard. "Ole Bull (1858)." In *Vienna's Golden Years of Music 1850-1900*. Penguin Books, Baltimore, Md., 1950.

Hassing, Arne. "Norway's Organized Response to Emigration." Norwegian-American Historical Association, Northfield, Minn., 1998.

Haugen, Einer, and Cai, Camilla. *Ole Bull: Norway's Romantic Musician and Cosmopolitan Patriot*, University of Wisconsin Press, Madison, Wisc.

Haugen, Einar. "Ole Bull and the Isles of Shoals." *The Norseman*, 1991.

Haugen, Einar. "Symra: A Memoir." Norwegian-American Historical Association, Northfield, Minn., 1972.

Hendriksen, Knut. *Ole Bull*. J. W. Cappelen Forlag, 2000

Herresthal, Harald. "The History of Music in Norway." *Nytt fra Norge* for the Ministry of Foreign Affairs, Oslo, Norway.

Hilen, Andrew. *Longfellow and Scandinavia: A Study of the Poet's Relationship with the Northern Languages and Literature*. New Haven, Conn., 1947.

Hopp, Zinken. *Eventyret om Ole Bull*. Bergen, Norway, 1945.

Horton, John. *Grieg*. London, 1974.

Hustvedt, Lloyd. *Rasmus Bjorn Anderson: Pioneer Scholar*. Northfield, Minn., 1966.

Jacobs, Stanley S. "The Violinist Who Thrilled Your Great-Grandmother." *Etude,* 1947.

Jahr, Torstein. "*Oleana*." Symra, 1910, Decorah, Iowa.

Janson, Kristofer. *The Spellbound Fiddler,* Chicago, 1880.

Jensen, Finn Robert. "Ole Bull, Nordmann Forut For Sin Tid."

Aftenposten, October 2000.

Johnsen, Birgit Hertzberg. "Norwegian Folktales and Legends," Ministry of Foreign Affairs, Norway.

Kelly, Bill. "Famed violin virtuoso, Ole Bull of Norway, has ties to Eau Claire." *Eau Claire Leader-Telegram*, Dec. 15, 1979.

Lande, Vidar. "Aakus, Eivind D., 1854-1937." *Slattar I tradisjon etter Meisterspelemanen*, 2001.

Lawrence, Vera Brodsky. *Strong on Music: The New York Music Scene in the Days of George Templeton Strong,* New York and Oxford, 1988.

Lessman, Otto. "How Ole Bull Made a Music Critic." *Musical America*, March 4, 1911.

Lie, Jonas. "Ole Bull, hans Karakteristik og Liv." Copenhagen, 1881

Linge, Ola. *Ole Bull: Livshistoria, Mannen, Kunstnaren*. Oslo, Norway, 1953.

Lloyd, Thomas W. and Charles T. Logue, with a preface by Henry W. Shoemaker, *Ole Bull in Pennsylvania: The Pilgrimage,* July 29, 1920, Pennsylvania, 1921.

Longfellow, Henry Wadsworth. *Tales of a Wayside Inn*. Boston, Mass., 1863.

Lovoll, Odd S. *The Promise of America: A History of the Norwegian-American People*. University of Minnesota Press, Minneapolis, Minn., 1984.

Lundeberg, Olav K. "Grandmother Sang for Ole Bull." *Lutheran Herald,* 1936

Meidell, Ditmar. "Oleana." *Krydseren*, March 5, 1853.

Meyer, Michael. *Ibsen, A Biography*. Garden City, N.Y., 1971.

Miller, Louise. "Weddings of the Past: Norwegian Violinist Weds American Girl." *La Crosse Sunday Tribune*, La Crosse, Wisc. May 14, 1967.

Moore, Aubertine Woodward (Auber Forestier). "The Real Ole Bull; Personal Reminiscences." *Etude,* 1912.

Moore, John W. "Ole Bull." *Western Musical World.* Ohio, May 1868.

Morgenbladet, Christiania/Oslo, Norway. Various articles.

"Museet Lysoen: Ole Bull's Home." *The Norway Post*, 1991.

New York Daily Times, New York, N.Y. Various articles.

"Norwegians in America." *New York Weekly Times.* Sept. 29-Oct. 2, 1852.

"Ole Bull: The Great Violinist Interviewed for the First Time." *New York Herald*, New York, N.Y., April 11, 1877.

People's Journal, Coudersport, Pa. Various articles, 1852-1853.

Pekarski, William J. "Ole Bull, Son of Norway," Indiana University of Pennsylvania, April 1993.

Philadelphia Press, Philadelphia, Pa. Various articles.

Potter County Journal, Coudersport, Pa. Various articles.

"Roster of Wisconsin Volunteers, War of the Rebellion, 1861-1865, Vol. 1, State of Wisconsin." Democrat Printing Company, Madison, Wisc., 1886.

Rynning, Ole. *True Account of America, 1838*. Beaver Creek, Ill.

Semmingsen, Ingrid Gaustad. "Norwegian Emigration to American During the 19th Century." Norwegian-American Historical Association, Northfield, Minn., 2001.

Shaw, John. "Norway, the International Citizen." *Diplomat*, August 2001.

Shoemaker, Henry W. "Memorials of Ole Bull and His Castle: They Should Be Gathered Before Too Late." *Altoona Tribune*, Altoona, Pa., May 30, 1941.

Simister, Frances, P. "The Ole Bull Place in West Lebanon." *Down East Enterprise*, 1970.

Skedsmo, Tone. "Knud Geelmuyden Bull," *Norsk Kunstner Leksikon*, Oslo, Norway, 1982.

Smith, Dexter. "Reminiscences of Ole Bull." *Boston Herald*. From archives of the New York Public Library.

Smith, Mortimer. *The Life of Ole Bull*, Princeton, N. J., 1943.

Snyder, Ole L. "The Ole Bull Colony." Paper read before the Potter County Historical Society, Coudersport, Pa., 1927.

Solberg, Carl Fredrik. "Reminiscences of a Pioneer Editor." Interview conducted July 25, 1919, at Milwaukee, Wisc.

Solem, Borge. "The Transatlantic Crossing." *100 Years of Emigrant Ships from Norway*. Translated to English by Harry T. Cleven. Norwegian National Library web presentation.

Stephenson, George M. "The Mind of the Scandinavian Immigrant." Norwegian-American Historical Assn., Northfield, Minn.

Stromme-Svendsen, Arnljot. "Ole Bull statuene og deres skapelse." *Bergens Tidende*, Sept. 30, 1980.

Thomas, Theodore. *A Musical Autobiography.* New York 1964.

Thompson, W. W. "Ole Borneman Bull." Assorted papers, Coudersport Pa.

Vik, Oddmund. *Ole Bull*, Bergen, Norway 1890.

Welfling, Mary E. *The Ole Bull Colony in Potter County.* Potter County Historical Society, Coudersport, Pa. 1952.

Wellauer, Maralyn. "Finding Norwegian Roots." *Family Chronicle*, May/June 2001.

Wiley, Byron. "Message from the President." Hardanger Fiddle Association of America Sound Post Archives, Internet, Spring 1999.

Wilkinson, Norman. *Ole Bull's New Norway.* Historical Pennsylvania Leaflet, No. 14, 1953. Rev. 1962 and 1988 by Robert Currin et al.

Wilson, James Grant. *Thackery in the United States, Vol. I*, New York, N,Y., 1904.

Winter-Hjelm, Henrik. "Traek af Ole Bulls Liv." *Morgenbladet*, 1852.

In addition to the sources listed above, the author obtained information in the archives of the Potter County Historical Society, in Coudersport Pa.; the University of Oslo Library, in Oslo, Norway; the Lysoen Museum on Lysoen Island near Bergen, Norway; the Smithsonian Institution and the Library of Congress, both in Washington D.C.; the Ole Bull Academy, in Voss, Norway; the Norwegian Emigrant Museum, near

Hamar, Norway; the Vesterheim Norwegian-American Museum, in Decorah, Iowa; and the Norwegian-American Historical Assn., in Northfield, Minn.